The Puffin
TREASURY
of
New Zealand
Children's Stories

PUFFIN BOOKS
Published by the Penguin Group
Penguin Group (NZ), 67 Apollo Drive, Rosedale,
North Shore 0632, New Zealand (a division of Pearson New Zealand Ltd)
Penguin Group (USA) Inc., 375 Hudson Street,
New York, New York 10014, USA
Penguin Group (Canada), 90 Eglinton Avenue East, Suite 700, Toronto,
Ontario, M4P 2Y3, Canada (a division of Pearson Penguin Canada Inc.)
Penguin Books Ltd, 80 Strand, London, WC2R 0RL, England
Penguin Ireland, 25 St Stephen's Green
Dublin 2, Ireland (a division of Penguin Books Ltd)
Penguin Group (Australia), 250 Camberwell Road, Camberwell,
Victoria 3124, Australia (a division of Pearson Australia Group Pty Ltd)
Penguin Books India Pvt Ltd, 11, Community Centre,
Panchsheel Park, New Delhi - 110 017, India
Penguin Books (South Africa) (Pty) Ltd, 24 Sturdee Avenue,
Rosebank, Johannesburg 2196, South Africa

Penguin Books Ltd, Registered Offices: 80 Strand, London, WC2R 0RL, England

First published by Viking/Penguin Books NZ, 1998
This edition published in Puffin Books NZ, 2004
10 9 8 7 6 5 4

This edition copyright © Penguin Books NZ, 1998
Stories selected and introduced by Jenni Keestra
Text and illustrations copyright © as listed in the acknowledgements on pages 277–278

Designed by Janine Brougham
Cover illustration by Simone End and design by Dexter Fry
Printed by Condor Production, Hong Kong

ISBN 978 014 33825 5
A catalogue record for this book is available
from the National Library of New Zealand.

www.penguin.co.nz

The Puffin TREASURY of New Zealand Children's Stories

Compiled by Jenni Keestra

PUFFIN BOOKS

CONTENTS

INTRODUCTION

Treasury.
A place where valuables are stored.
A collection of precious things.

New Zealand has its own treasure trove in its wonderful writers and illustrators, many of whom you will meet in this collection. They are the people who create the magic that can take you from your own world into the lives and experiences of others. You will probably already know some of their books. Surely everyone has encountered the fun and magic of Margaret Mahy's stories, or enjoyed the sparkle of Joy Cowley's writing, or laughed at one of William Taylor's outrageous tales. But if some of the writers here are new to you then you'll have all the pleasure of reading their work for the first time – and all the fun of going out and looking for more books by them.

You'll find all kinds of writing here – picture books, poems, short stories and extracts from longer books. You'll meet all kinds of people, too. Some are living ordinary, everyday lives. You might recognise yourself, or your friends and family, in their stories. Others are extraordinary, fantastic people who invite you to visit astonishing places and share their adventures. Have you ever been given something horrible to eat in a restaurant, or had to do something that terrifies you? Do you have a piece of clothing you like so much you don't ever want to throw it away? Have you daydreamed about magical journeys and saving the world? Have you wondered what it would be like to live in the days before cars, television and computers? Books let you explore anywhere and anything you want to.

The Puffin Treasury of New Zealand Children's Stories is packed with words, but it's also full of pictures by New Zealand's talented artists. Most of the illustrations belong to the original story, and you'll recognise Robyn Belton's brave little bantam hen and Lynley Dodd's determined turtle. Some other illustrations have been drawn especially for this treasury and you can enjoy the very fine artwork alongside the stories and poems.

All of this belongs to you. When you begin reading you will become part of the story, and the story will become part of you. Turn the page. Begin the adventure.

Gwenda Turner

OVER ON THE FARM

ILLUSTRATED BY GWENDA TURNER

Over on the farm
in the summer sun
Lived an old mother cow
and her little calf

one

Moo said the mother
We moo said the one
So they mooed all day
in the summer sun.

1

1

Over on the farm
by the barn painted blue
Lived an old mother sheep
and her little lambs

two

Baa said the mother
We baa said the two
So they bleated all day
by the barn painted blue.

2

1   **2**

Over on the farm
in the walnut tree
Lived an old mother sparrow
and her little sparrows

three

Chirrup said the mother
We chirrup said the three
So they chirruped all day
in the walnut tree.

3

Over on the farm
by the farmhouse door
Lived an old mother cat
and her little kittens

four

Miaow said the mother
We miaow said the four
So they miaowed all day
by the farmhouse door.

4

1

2

3

4

Over on the farm
where the small fish dive
Lived an old mother frog
and her tadpoles
five
Swim said the mother
We swim said the five
So they swam all day
where the small fish dive.

5

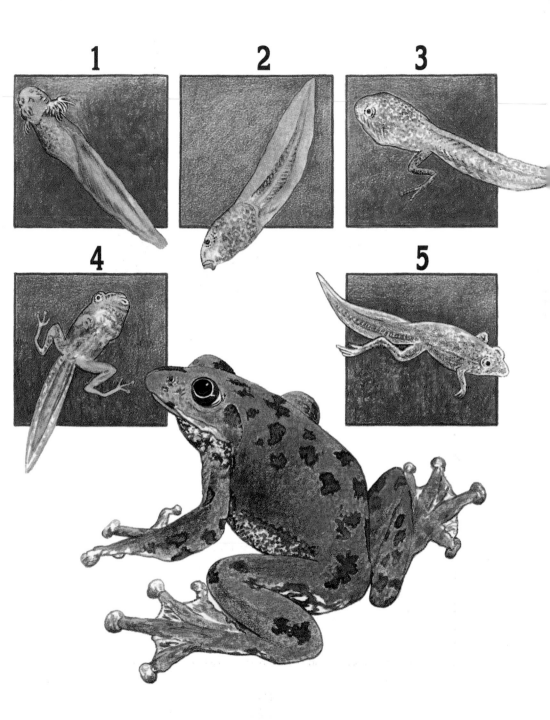

Over on the farm
in a sty built of sticks
Lived an old mother pig
and her little piglets

six

Oink said the mother
We oink said the six
So they oinked all day
in a sty built of sticks.

6

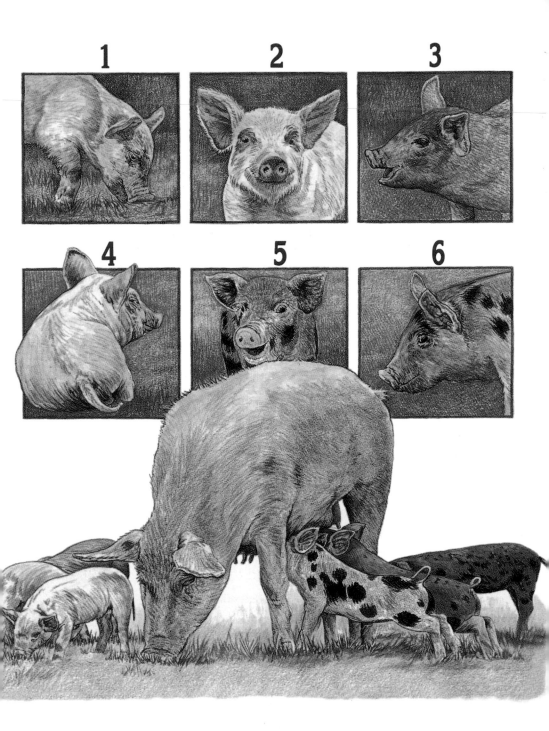

Over on the farm
in a roost named heaven
Lived an old mother hen
and her little chicks

seven

Cheep said the mother
We cheep said the seven
So they cheeped all day
in a roost named heaven.

7

Over on the farm
by the old wooden gate
Lived an old mother duck
and her little ducklings

eight

Quack said the mother
We quack said the eight
So they quacked all day
by the old wooden gate.

8

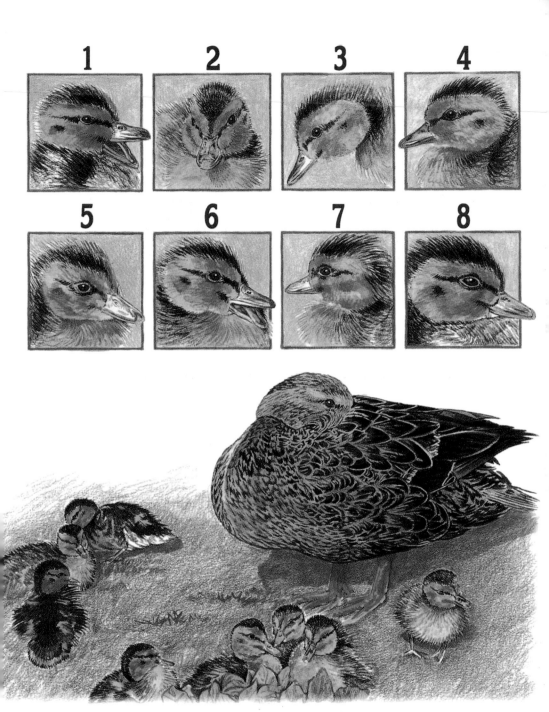

Over on the farm
under the dark green pine
Lived an old mother hedgehog
and her little hedgehogs

nine

Sniff said the mother
We sniff said the nine
So they sniffed all day
under the dark green pine.

9

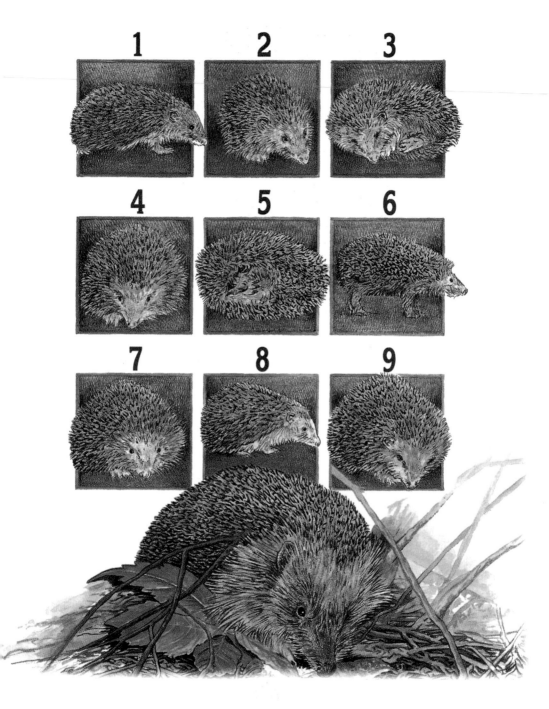

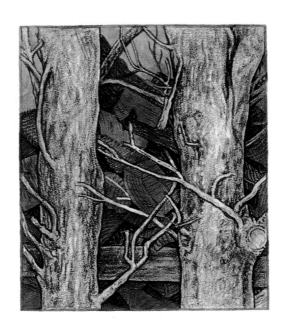

Over on the farm
in a snug wee den
Lived an old mother mouse
and her little mice

ten

Squeak said the mother
We squeak said the ten
So they squeaked all day
in a snug wee den.

10

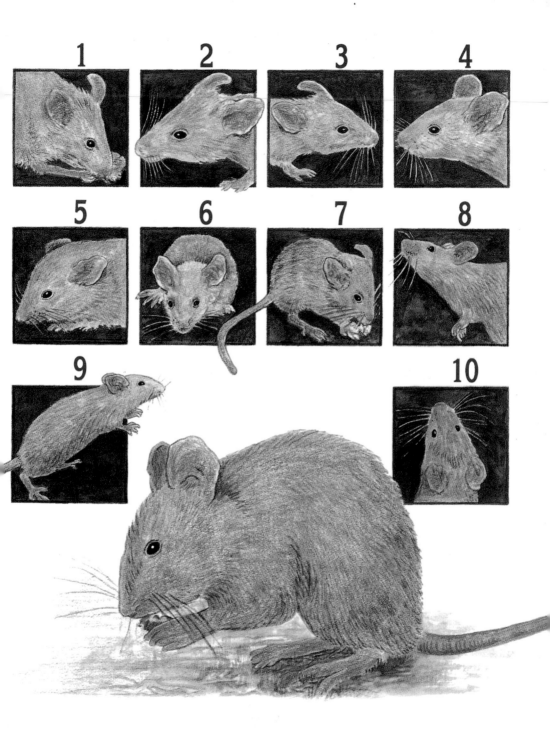

Gavin Bishop

BIDIBIDI

ILLUSTRATED BY GAVIN BISHOP

It was a hot and windless day in the mountains. The large flock of sheep was searching for grass amongst the rocks and spiky spaniard plants. 'My feet are sore,' said Bidibidi. 'I'm tired of trudging around these bony mountains just to fill my stomach.' She sat down and stared into the distance where a rainbow sprang into the air. 'That's where I want to be,' thought Bidibidi.

'You'll get left behind,' said a shrill voice behind her. It was Stella the kea. 'Go away!' muttered Bidibidi crossly. 'Just being friendly,' said Stella. 'I'm sorry,' said Bidibidi, 'I'm so tired of wandering around, nibbling here, nibbling there, sore feet, nasty thorns, day after day.' 'If you're not happy with your life, do something about it,' said Stella. 'I don't know what else there is.'

'You'll never know unless you go and find out,' said Stella. Bidibidi thought for a moment. She looked at the rainbow in the distance. 'Where do I go?' she asked. 'Down,' said Stella.

And so Bidibidi set off down the mountainside.

By mid-day it was hot and sunny. Bidibidi rested for a while in the shade of some trees by a rocky stream. In the cool gloom she dozed off, dreaming of the rainbow.

Soon she was interrupted. Some of Stella's friends were shouting from the tree-tops.
'Turn right at the great waters.'
'Take care at the deserted hotel.'

'Beware the wire with claws.'

Bidibidi looked up. 'Wire with claws? Deserted hotel? Great waters?' she cried. The keas rose into the air and flew off towards the higher slopes. Bidibidi continued her journey, following the stream. It became wider and deeper. The beds of shingle on each side were strewn with the bleached remains of tree trunks. Strange birds fled as she approached. Following a bend in the river, Bidibidi found an expanse of sparkling blue water, more water than she had seen in her life. 'The great waters! I must turn right.' As Bidibidi was clattering along the stones at the lake's edge she noticed a slight movement in the reeds nearby. She stopped. A large bird sat with its beak in the air, blending perfectly with the reeds and grasses.

'Go away,' it hissed. 'You're not supposed to see me.'

'Oh, excuse me,' said Bidibidi, 'I don't want to disturb you, but I don't know where to go from here.'

'Lake,' spat the bittern.

'How? I can't fly or swim,' said Bidibidi.

'Float!'

'I don't,' Bidibidi was alarmed.

'Boat.'

'Boat?' repeated Bidibidi. The bittern rolled her eyes impatiently. In no time she picked a pile of bulrushes and began to weave and plait a small boat. Half an hour later she hustled Bidibidi on board, without so much as a few words of good luck. A shrill whistle from the bittern brought a large brown trout to the shore. Bidibidi just had time to say thank you before the fish towed her craft towards the centre of the lake.

'Where are you taking me?' called Bidibidi. The trout didn't answer.

A gentle breeze began to blow and the little boat bobbed up and down on a slight swell. With the warm sun and the gentle rocking, Bidibidi was soon asleep. Suddenly Bidibidi was awake. She was wet!

'I'm sinking! Help!' she bleated. The boat was leaking. Water lapped her knees. 'Help! Help!' The trout continued to tow her boat. The water reached her stomach. 'I wish I was high and dry on my mountainside,' she moaned. 'Oh, please help!' At last Bidibidi was heard by some ducks.

'Come on, boys. To the rescue!' called a young mallard drake. Before Bidibidi knew what was happening, she was lifted into the air and whisked across the lake to land.

When she had recovered her breath, Bidibidi left the lake and continued to travel further and further away from the mountains. Tussock gave way to grassland and clumps of shelter trees. At dusk, she came across a strange sight. In a clump of dark pine trees stood a large wooden building. Over the doorway was a sign:

LEG O' MUTTON ARMS
ESTABLISHED
– 1870 –

It was the deserted hotel.

Bidibidi nervously settled down under the trees. She managed to drift into a restless sleep but awoke often to cast a glance at the old hotel. A night wind made the pines creak and crack above her head.

At midnight a shout of laughter woke Bidibidi. Roving lights lit up the windows of the old hotel, and the notes of a honky-tonk piano echoed from the empty shell. Bidibidi jumped up and took off in fright. Through the trees she ran, over rabbit-cropped turf, down gullies, up the other side. Suddenly she was brought to a violent halt, fiercely clutched by the wool on her back. Bidibidi fought her invisible attacker but the grip on her fleece grew even tighter.

By the pale light of dawn she saw what had trapped her. 'The wire with claws,' she bleated feebly, thinking of the keas' warning. All day she lay there, unable to escape. 'I'll have you free in a jiffy,' said a husky voice from behind her. 'Maxine hound at your service.' The sheep-dog bit and clawed, releasing Bidibidi from the barbed wire. 'Come home and stay with me,' she offered. 'I'd like that,' said Bidibidi.

Bidibidi squeezed into Maxine's kennel and fell asleep beside her new friend. She woke some time later, cold and alone. Maxine was gone. The lights were on in the farmhouse. Bidibidi left the kennel and trotted up to the house. Black shapes moved across the blind.

She could hear voices. 'Have a nice bit of lamb, Maxine,' someone said. Bidibidi froze. This was no place for her. Bidibidi ran from the farmhouse as fast as she could, on and on through the night. 'I am going to go home,' she panted.

Morning was late in arriving. The sky was dark and cloudy and Bidibidi heard the descending notes of the grey warbler. A thunderstorm was brewing in the hills ahead. As she ran for shelter the storm suddenly crashed around her. Lightning flashed, and the thunder shook her empty belly. A torrent of water blocked the entrance to her shelter. Gradually the storm grew quiet and the rain

stopped. A crescent of coloured light leapt from a rock and soared through the parting clouds down into a distant valley. Delicate tinkling sounds filtered through the moist and sparkling air.

Bidibidi scrambled up the rocks to find an old man with a fuzzy white beard. He was dressed in clothes the colour of the hills and on his head was an extraordinary hat. Hanging at his side was an old hurdy-gurdy. 'Rainbow Jackson's the name,' he said. 'I make all the rainbows with this old machine of mine.' He patted the box. 'You're wet. Come and have a warm by my fire.' The old man's hut was warm and cosy. Bidibidi dried off in front of the fire. 'Why don't you stay for a while,' asked Rainbow Jackson. 'I could do with some company.'

So Bidibidi did stay, and in fact she never left. She stayed on through the rest of the summer helping to plan the rainbow displays that were needed after thunderstorms. She stayed on through the autumn when the wind brought the promise of snow. During the long winter nights, she slept safe and warm in front of the fire. And she was there in the spring when the ranunculae and gentians flowered amongst the sweet mountain grass.

When Rainbow Jackson grew very old he gave Bidibidi his hurdy-gurdy.

'I'll make the rainbows now,' she said.

And that's what Bidibidi did.

Robyn Kahukiwa

TANIWHA

ILLUSTRATED BY ROBYN KAHUKIWA

There's a taniwha in my river.
People say it's a log, but I know it's a taniwha.
She's been in my river a long time.

Before I was alive, and before my koro was alive,
the taniwha was in my river.

Sometimes she talks to me.

Sometimes I ride on her back
and she takes me places.
She tells me stories about the old days
when people lived close to the land.

The taniwha warned our tribe of danger and death.
They listened to her then.

Once we flew across the trees to the sea.
We dived down, down into the water
and saw Tangaroa and his children.
The taniwha found a shiny green stone
and gave it to me to keep.

Once we flew to Ranginui,
up, up, up into the highest cloud.
On top of the cloud we saw a hokioi bird in her nest.

The taniwha found a fluffy white feather
and gave it to me to keep.

Once we flew to the other side of Papatuanuku
and saw her baby, Ruaumoko.

The taniwha found some soft red earth
and gave it to me to keep.

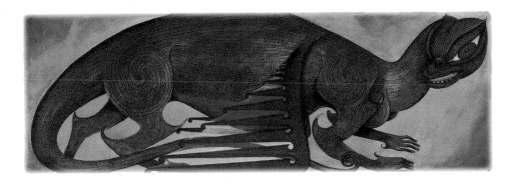

I showed the gifts to a friend.
He looked and laughed.
'A stone, a feather and dirt?
What rubbish!'

I showed the gifts to my koro.
He looked and smiled.
'You have seen the faces of Tangaroa,
Ranginui and Papatuanuku.
How rich you are!'

There's a taniwha in my river.
People say it's a log, but I know it's a taniwha.

taniwha:	legendary monster
koro:	old man, grandfather
Tangaroa:	God of the ocean
Ranginui:	Skyfather
Papatuanuku:	Earthmother
Ruaumoko:	baby of Papatuanuku and Ranginui
hokioi:	fabulous bird

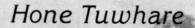

Hone Tuwhare

HAIKU

Stop
your snivelling
creek-bed:

come rain hail
and flood-water

laugh again

Margaret Mahy

The Man
from the Land
of Fandango

ILLUSTRATED BY QUENTIN BLAKE

The man from the land of Fandango
Is coming to pay you a call,
With his tricolour jacket and polka-dot tie
And his calico trousers as blue as the sky
And his hat with a tassel and all.
And he bingles and bangles and bounces,
He's a bird! He's a bell! He's a ball!
The man from the land of Fandango
Is coming to pay you a call.

Oh, whenever they dance in Fandango
   The bears and the bison join in,
And baboons with bassoons make a musical sound.
   And the kangaroos come with a hop and a bound,
And the dinosaurs join in the din,
   And they tingle and tongle and tangle
Till tomorrow turns into today.
   Then they stop for a break and a drink and a cake
In their friendly fandandical way.

The man from the land of Fandango
   Is given to dancing and dreams.
He comes in at the door like a somersault star
   And he juggles with junkets and jam in a jar
And custards and caramel creams.
   And he jingles and jongles and jangles
As he dances on ceilings and walls,
   And he only appears every five hundred years
So you'd better be home when he calls.

Hone Tuwhare

BIRD OF PRAYER

On the skyline
a hawk
languidly typing
a hunting poem
with its wings

Ruth Dallas

SHINING RIVERS

ILLUSTRATED BY GARETH FLOYD

Fourteen-year-old Johnie Crawford gets caught up in the gold rush and gold fever that is mounting in the town.

T ravelling by night was very slow, but gradually the sky lightened and the sun came up in a clear sky and shone on the tops of the hills that surrounded us. There was no road, no track, no fence, no house, no tree in that lonely landscape. The only vegetation was the New Zealand tussock and thorny bushes which grew among great rough rocks.

Tatey wanted to put the greatest distance possible between ourselves and the gully we had left, so we kept on till I felt my legs trembling from hunger and weariness and asked him when we were going to have breakfast. We had climbed down into a pass, by that time, where a little stream ran over stones, and there, hidden between two great rocks as big as houses, we fried some bacon in the pan and then boiled water in the same pan and drank it scalding hot. Tatey took care to hide the evidence of our fire and we pressed on, sleeping that night in the tussocks in the shelter of rocks.

Rocks had become the main feature of the landscape, some standing in clusters as though meeting to discuss the intrusion of two fly-like human beings on their territory. Some were in long ridges, like petrified railway carriages. Some had mats of tussock on their heads like wigs. It was desert country, steep country, a mad kind of country, only fit for madmen in search of gold.

Tatey was a little ahead of me. I was tramping along behind him. At the top of a hill he paused and told me to look down. In the next valley I could see the gleam of water like a knife blade. A stream wound along the valley floor, a mere ribbon of water, running over a wide area of bare mountain shingle, sometimes hidden, and sometimes showing up further on.

'No one's been here,' Tatey said, 'ever.' And he began to hurry down the steep hillside as though in competition with other men who might reach the stream first.

'This is the spot,' he said, setting down the cradle at the waterside. I, too, set down my swag, and was very glad to do so. I could see no sign of Tatey's having staked out a claim, or of a pit where he had been digging. The stony valley was bare and desolate and we were enclosed by a complete circle of bare hills. The water made a musical sound as it ran over the stones. To my great amazement Tatey seized the frying pan and walked into the water without taking his boots off, and, with his bare hands, began to scoop gravel from the bottom of the river into the pan, and to wash it, where he stood. Then he carried the pan out to me and I could see gold shining on the bottom as though it had been spilt there.

We stared at the gold and looked into each other's faces, neither of us able to speak. I had imagined that men jumped for joy when they found gold. Instead, I found tears blurring my vision.

'There's a bar,' Tatey said at last, 'a river bar – it's caught on the bar – every time I put down my shovel –'

He set up the cradle and fell to feeding it with river gravel and water and rocking it with my enthusiastic assistance and before long we had washed up nearly two ounces.

I couldn't understand this method of mining gold. I thought it had to be dug out of a hole in the ground and I told Tatey so.

'If it's been buried by floods since the beginning of time, of course you have to dig for it,' Tatey said. 'That's how we got it in Victoria. But this is not Australia, it's New Zealand, and if we're going to get gold in the rivers as well as in the ground our fortune's made.'

When the sun disappeared behind the hills the valley grew very cold and I asked Tatey if his feet were not cold, since his boots and trouser legs were wet and he was still walking in and out of the river.

'Didn't know I had feet,' he said. 'I'm not giving up this game till dark. When our friends back in Gabriel's Gully find out we've gone they're going to come and look for us, especially when they find out we made a midnight flit.'

'Do you think they'll find us?'

'I'm not waiting to see,' Tatey said. 'I'm going to scratch up and down this river while the going's good. And turn out first thing in the morning, too, use all the hours of daylight. If we get a rush we'll be confined to a twenty-four foot claim and our fortune will be gone.'

At length it grew too dark to see what we were doing, so we retired to a sheltered place among the rocks that jutted from the foot of the hillside, where Tatey had left his calico tent and other gear he had taken on his prospecting trip. We built a fire from sticks we had gathered in the river bed and cooked a meal and Tatey dried his wet boots on warmed stones.

Those were the last days of autumn, sunny and short, with clear blue skies, and with a full moon at night, and stars sparkling in the first light frosts. I kept my clothes on for warmth and rolled myself in my blanket. When I closed my eyes I saw gold, flakes, crumbs, nuggets. Tatey had estimated that we had washed up about five ounces.

'Where are we going to hide it?' I asked him.

'Where you'd least expect to find it,' he said. 'We'll think of something.' Then he said, 'To think it was lying here all the time while we were working like convicts back at Gabriel's! It's been lying here for centuries!'

'Has this valley got a name?'

'You name it.'

I fell asleep trying to think of a name for it, but in the morning noticed a tall rock that was like the chimney that is left standing when a house has been burnt down, and called it Chimney Gully, which was a bit of a joke, because that valley had never seen a real chimney.

The small bar in the river where Tatey first found gold was worked out on the second day, and we had to look elsewhere, but Tatey knew where to look, and as we had the river to ourselves we went upstream and found more gold. While I worked the cradle I kept watching the hills to see whether anyone else was coming into the valley. At first the hills seemed sinister, a threat to our security, but when no one came I began to grow tense, and wished someone would come and put an end to the waiting. I found the loneliness, after the crowd at Gabriel's, hard to endure. I saw the sun come up and I saw it go down, and I saw the moon pass, but nothing else passed, unless you counted the wind, which often blew in the tussocks. It may sound strange, but I formed a kind of friendship with the stream, which was a river, really, low because of the fine autumn weather.

The river was always busy, and its voice was cheerful, as though it sang, and it was full of coloured stones, as well as gold. The stones were green or red or marble-white or speckled. The water was crystal clear and no matter how often we muddied it, the mud would settle and the water run clear again. The water was lovely to drink and made the best tea I have ever tasted. We washed in it, we ill-treated it, we stole from it, but it still ran clear and sang. Of course I said nothing of this to Tatey, who would have thought I was as mad as a hatter, and I didn't notice the river so much after Dan and Rex came.

Yes, they spotted us from the hilltops, and came scrambling down, and worked like beavers and they got so much gold their behaviour became rather peculiar, in that they became exaggeratedly secretive.

They set up camp near us, but no longer played cards with Tatey. They evidently thought there was more gold to be won from the river than to be won from Tatey, and, like us, they worked all the

daylight hours, and slept like dead men at night. We were all on limited food supplies and knew that when the food we had brought with us was consumed we would have to return to the store at Gabriel's for more, taking gold dust with us to buy it, and that it would be very difficult to get back to Chimney Gully without being followed.

Tatey was disappointed in that nowhere along the river could he find a pocket of gold as rich as the first he had found. The small river bar, which was almost a bridge of rocks, had acted as a check to the flow of the water for centuries, and there the gold had settled. We dug all round it, but it turned out to be one of those freak surprises that rivers give miners as though to mock them. We found the colour elsewhere, but it soon became apparent that we would have to find more than the colour to make it worth while staying in that valley.

Tatey, Dan and Rex had an inclination to work upstream knowing that the gold had come from the inland mountains in the first place, but one day without giving it any thought, I took a pan and shovel and made my way downstream and made an astonishing discovery.

In that lonely valley, far from the habitation of man, I came across a tent, erected on the river bank. Nothing could have given me a greater surprise. Beside the tent a pit had been dug in the shingle, in the manner of the pits we had dug at Gabriel's. But Tatey had explained to me that pits were for gold that had been buried under centuries of rubble, and that in this valley the gold was in the river.

I had now been so long with the miners that I had become like them, cautious and suspicious, and had learnt to hide from others my activities, so I sat down among the tussocks and kept watch on the camp. I knew that intruders on what we considered 'our' valley was the last thing the men wanted. I also knew that if I betrayed our position I would be given a very rough time.

I waited a long time in the tussocks, thinking the unknown miners might be down the river, or, if they were anywhere near, I would hear some sound that would indicate their position. But all I could hear was the cheerful sound of the water running over the stones, and the lonely sound of the wind in the tussocks. There was no sound of bird or insect. The sky was a flawless bright blue, with no wisp of cloud on the hills, and the dry shingle shone white in the sun.

After a while it occurred to me that the tent had been very badly set up, since it sagged, and flapped in the light wind that was travelling along the valley. It was a simple sheet of calico draped over the dead branches of a great tree that had been washed down the river in a flood. A fireplace had been built against the prostrate trunk of the tree, and flames had charred it. But the fireplace of stones had a dead appearance and seemed dusted over with sand, as though the wind had been blowing over it, and I began to wonder if the camp was deserted.

I now debated with myself whether I ought to investigate further. If there were miners working here I thought Tatey and the others ought to know, so that we could keep upstream and out of their way. If they did not find gold themselves and did not discover us, they would move on. But if I found the camp deserted, well then, I could carry on with my original purpose, of prospecting downstream. I had dreams of finding another river bar, like the one Tatey had found at first, where you only had to put down your shovel to bring up gold.

When I weighed my thoughts in the balance like this, the gold always weighed heavier, and decided my actions, because I still had the gold fever. So I went down to the tent and looked inside.

Joy Cowley

BOW DOWN
SHADRACH

ILLUSTRATED BY JOHN HURFORD

*Shadrach is a very old, circus-trained Clydesdale
horse – and the favourite family pet.*

They went along another sheep track which cut across the side of the hill and wound down to a little gully at the back of the house. They'd put Shadrach there last week because the feed was better than in his usual house paddock. The gully was the most fertile spot on the farm and grass grew as thick as hair with clumps of buttercups in the damp patches.

Hannah put her fingers in her mouth and whistled.

'Oh!' cried Eliana. 'Do show me how you do that!'

The moment was lost however, for there was an immediate answer from under the trees, an eager noise whiffling through the nostrils and lips of the old draughthorse as he came lumbering out in something between a trot and a hobble. He went immediately to Hannah, nuzzling against her face, her hair. Hannah glanced back at Eliana and explained, 'He's very very old.'

Eliana didn't speak. She simply looked, her mouth half open.

Hannah hugged Shadrach's neck, filling herself with the smell of him and telling him fiercely that he was beautiful, beautiful. But at the same time she could see him through Eliana's eyes, an old arthritic horse with the bones sticking out of his coat, a hairy protruding lower lip which hung open showing stumps of yellow teeth. She screwed up her eyes. What was it about Eliana that made everything seem so ordinary?

'Did you say his name is Shadrach?' Eliana asked.

'Yes.'

'That's in the Bible.'

'I know.'

'What about all these tricks he's supposed to do?'

'It's not a matter of "Suppose",' cried Hannah. 'He really does do tricks. Years and years ago he belonged to a circus. There were three Clydesdale stallions and their names were Shadrach, Meshach and . . . and . . .'

'Abednego,' said Eliana.

'Yes. They were called after the three men in the story about the fiery furnace. These men wouldn't bow down to the statue of the king so they got thrown into a huge bonfire.'

'But they didn't get burned,' said Eliana.

'The circus act was taken off that story. Joe told me about it. There was this man dressed up as a king and he would say, "Come to me, Shadrach. Come to me, Meshach. Come to me . . . um . . ."'

'Abednego.'

'You know what would happen? The horses would walk backwards away from him. Then he'd shout, "Don't you walk away! Look me in the eye!" That's when the horses would turn their backs to him and flick their tails. Everyone laughed, Joe said. So then the king got really mad and he yelled to each one of them, "Bow down!" Every time he told them to bow down, they'd rear up on their hind legs. In the end he got so angry he said they had to go into the fiery furnace.'

'Not real fire!' said Eliana.

'Yes, real fire. There was a big burning hoop and the stallions had to jump through it.'

'How utterly cruel!' Eliana said.

Hannah smiled at her, warming to the emotion in her voice. She rubbed Shadrach's whiskery nose. 'It was awful, that's for sure. Some circuses used to do terrible things to animals, Joe said. But the Society for the Prevention of Cruelty to Animals stopped the act and the circus had to sell three Clydesdale horses who'd been trained to do the opposite of what they were told. You watch this.' Hannah stepped back from Shadrach and said, 'Look me in the eye!'

The old horse came forward and nudged at her hand for a piece of apple or a sugar cube.

'No, Shadrach!' Hannah stepped back again. 'Look me in the eye!'

He paused like a stuck wind-up toy, then he sidestepped in a circle until his tail was presented to Hannah.

Eliana clapped her hands. 'That's clever!'

Hannah went round Shadrach and kissed him on the nose. 'Sophie and Joe bought him the year before I was born. That's how long we've had him. They thought he'd be good for a plough and cart but Shadrach had other ideas. Joe says there was no way he could make him work. But he was really good with children. Only a year ago we were still riding him to school, Mikey and I. On the way home, if he got hot, he'd go into the sea with us on his back. But he's too old for riding now.'

'Does he still remember the other circus tricks?' Eliana wanted to know.

'You bet he does. You're really magic, aren't you, Shadrach?'

'Can he still bow down?'

'Of course! He hasn't done it for ages but he still remembers.' Hannah stepped well away from him and called out loudly, 'Bow down, Shadrach!'

He tossed his head a little and flicked his tail at the flies which settled on his flanks. Sweat made his coat shine as though it had been oiled.

'Bow down, Shadrach!'

He knew the words and he whinnied, shuffled, gathered energy for his response.

'Bow down, Shadrach!' Hannah shouted.

He seemed to be drawing strength into himself, tensing his muscles. His head went back and the next thing he was up, his great hairy fetlocks pawing at the air, his hind legs shifting about in the grass. Up he stayed, his eyes rolling with the effort of it, and then suddenly he fell. Instead of coming down on all fours, he went sideways, his body hitting the ground. The sound was like that of a falling tree.

Neither Hannah nor Eliana moved.

Shadrach seemed dead. His eye was turned so far back it showed only red. A muscle twitched in his leg but apart from that he wasn't moving, wasn't breathing. Then, after a long time, there was a noisy pull of air into his lungs. He shuddered and gave another deep gasp.

Hannah got down on the ground and tried to lift his head. 'Shadrach!'

The shuddering, twitching movements increased and he tried to sit up. His legs flailed uselessly as though he no longer knew what they were for, and he lay flat again.

Eliana said in her matter-of-fact way, 'He's probably got a broken leg!'

The words brought such a huge pain to Hannah that she couldn't speak. She knew that if it were true, Shadrach would have to be shot, and it would be her fault.

'Do you want me to go and get someone?' Eliana offered.

Hannah nodded, stroking Shadrach's muzzle. Then, as soon as Eliana was on her way to the house, she started to cry.

Ron Bacon

AGAIN THE BUGLES BLOW

ILLUSTRATED BY V. J. LIVINGSTON

Rua pressed himself harder into the earth.
He heard voices again, calling softly, and for a moment
his heart stopped . . .

It was dark. Mostly it was quiet, so the sound of moreporks calling in the trees across the valley sounded clear on the night air, but every now and then a musket would fire, and as if it was a signal, there'd be a scattering of shots and bullets would sing overhead or thud into the tight bundled sap-rollers. At first Rua had ducked when bullets had splintered into the rollers, but after a while he realised that by the time he heard the bullets it was too late to duck so now he just kept on digging. The men in the sap worked without sound except for an occasional remark and a grunted reply, but from the pa on the hill there came an endless wailing, sometimes loud and shrill, sometimes soft and mournfully low. It went on and on, the terrible crying of the women in the pa.

'Will you hear them poor souls,' said a soldier, pausing to listen.

'Aye,' said another, ' 'tis a bad thing we do.'

'Dig,' said the first, 'dig, and get this devil's work done,' and they bent again to their shovels.

Rua's chance came when the next group of men came along the sap to take their turn at digging. They stumbled along the trench in the darkness, there were a few softly spoken words and the men Rua had been working with handed over their shovels, and quietly, heads down, went back along the sap. Rua went more slowly, dragging behind the others until he was alone, and then he was scrambling up the side of the sap.

The soft soil slid under his feet, but he scratched and clawed his way until he was out and running up the hill slope. There was a shout from behind and then a musket shot, and then it was as if every gun was being fired at once. He flung himself flat on the grass, pressing tight to the ground, trying to force himself into the earth, until suddenly the firing stopped and the only sound was the wailing from up the hill.

Rua stayed still, listening and waiting, but there were no more shots and when the morepork called again from over the valley, he carefully stretched out a hand and pulled himself a little farther up the slope, still pressing himself hard against the dew-wet grass. He didn't know how far he was from the pa, but slowly he worked his way forward, ready all the time to stop and lie still, or to jump up and run back, into the covering darkness.

And then, through the sound of the wailing, he could hear soft voices. He lifted his head and there was a darker shadow against the dark sky. It was the earth wall around the pa.

Rua stayed still. This was going to be the hardest part, getting over that mound of earth without being seen by the warriors watching and waiting on the other side.

He didn't move. What would happen if a Kingite sentry heard the grass rustle and thought he was a soldier? A hundred muskets would blaze out, a hundred tomahawks would slash down . . .

Rua pressed himself harder into the earth.

He heard voices again, calling softly, and for a moment his heart stopped. The voices were behind him, down the hill, low Maori voices that called again and were answered softly from within the pa.

He clutched the short grass and lay, too frightened to breathe.

There was the whisper of grass against bare feet and the sound of breathing. He could almost feel someone bending over him. It was too late to run, too late to say anything, too late to do anything. There were two men – he could feel one on either side. Someone called again, a question, from the wall of the pa, and one of the men answered in a soft whisper, and then they were standing straight, talking softly. Someone else was coming over the wall, one or two people, and now they were all standing by Rua, murmuring to one another.

And just when Rua was sure he'd have to cry out, 'Please, I'm not an enemy! I don't even belong here!' from down the hill came a musket shot and at once the night was loud with guns, from the soldiers and from the pa.

Rua never quite knew what happened next, it was all over so quickly. He heard the men around him gasp, then they yelled and were gone, running for the pa. But before they were over, Rua was on his feet, scrambling up with them, over the wall, tumbling down the other side in a flurry of arms and legs, into the pa.

Sherryl Jordan

DENZIL'S DILEMMA

*Denzil gets tangled more and more in the web
of his own making . . .*

Denzil stood in the snow behind Valvasor's house, the parchment clutched in his hands, and stared. The snow was brilliant. White light shone all around, so bright it almost blinded him. Glorious it was, unearthly and shimmering, and warm. Then, out of the very heart of the light, her hair golden and her face full of joy, came Sam. Sam with a white gown and angel's wings.

'Oh, gawd!' howled Denzil, horrified. 'I've killed her! Oh, sweet Jesus, Mother Mary, Saint Theresa! Save me! I've done a wicked murder!' And he fell on the ground, sobbing.

Bewildered, Sam watched him for a while, wondering where she was. Freezing wind hissed across her bare arms, and her feet ached in the whiteness on the ground. She felt dizzy with the cold, and her eyes could hardly bear the brightness all around. After a few moments she realised that she stood in snow. And there was a great stone house behind Denzil; a house with wooden shutters instead of glass in the windows, and a thatched roof dripping melted snow and icicles.

'You've brought me to your world,' she said, amazed, half smiling.

lowly, Denzil lifted his head. His face was as pale as the paper he held crushed to his chest. His hands shook. Sam inspected him, noticing that he'd grown a bit. He was wearing a tough woven brown tunic, and handmade leather shoes with long pointed toes. He had a grey hat with a peak dangling down the back, and it fitted right around his face like a balaclava, with a wide collar that covered his shoulders. His thin legs were covered with woollen grey hose, patched on the knees with dirty yellow squares.

Sam grinned. 'I suppose the pink tights don't fit you anymore,' she said.

Denzil gulped. 'I'm sorry, Sam,' he choked. 'Please forgive me.'

'Doesn't worry me,' she said. 'You looked silly in ballet tights, anyway.'

'Not the tights. You. I'm sorry about you.'

Sam's grin vanished. 'What do you mean, sorry?' She was quiet for a while, staring at him, while a fear colder than the snow settled across her heart.

'Are you telling me that this is a mistake?' she asked. 'That I'm not supposed to be here, after all? That you've been dabbling in spells too big for you, and now it's my turn to be stuck somewhere hundreds of years away from home?'

Denzil shrank back against the stone wall. 'Don't be angry, Sam,' he whimpered. 'Please. I didn't know. I must have got it wrong again. I . . .' Sam's blue eyes narrowed. Murgatroyd squeaked in her hands, and she put him up onto her left shoulder. He sat there shivering. Sam had been shivering too, a second ago, but now she felt hot with rage.

f you've messed things up again, Denzil, I'll make you really sorry. Mum's supposed to be taking a photo of me. It takes her half an hour to get that camera sorted out, and just when she finally gets it right, I disappear. That's rotten timing. I thought you'd be a better wizard by now. I thought you'd have your spells sorted out – have your magic a bit more under control. Well, you're just as bad at it as ever.'

'And you're just as snappish as ever, Sammy Snarlybritches!' he yelled, standing up, and going over to face her. 'I bet you're not even a good angel! I bet they've got a special place for crosspatches like you, somewhere just inside the Pearly Gates, where nobody stays for long! I bet you don't even get to see the saints! I bet they make you polish the harps! I bet –'

'I'm not an angel!' she cried. 'I'm me! Sam!'

One day Sherryl Jordan was talking to her frend, Jean Bennett. (Sherry's the one who holds the pen— I'm the wizzard who makes the reel magic). They wer talking about me and Jean sed: "Woodnt it bee fun if Denzil took Sam back to his wirld."

I got reely exited about that idea — I'd thawt about it my-self a few times. Luckilee Sherryl got exited about it too and between us we got Sam back to my place. We had a marveliss time even thow things did get a little bit out of control.

I'm writting this to thank Jean for her wunderfol idea.

Thank yoo Jean.

With greetings from

Denzil

'Didn't think you were!' he sniffed. 'Your wings are falling off. They haven't got real feathers, either. Bet you can't even fly as well as I can.'

'I can't fly at all,' she said, wriggling her shoulders where the straps were slipping. 'I'm not an angel, Denzil. I'm just dressed up as one for our school play. The wings are make-believe. Mum made them for me.'

'You're not dead then?'

'I hope not. I thought I was just visiting you. Isn't this your world?'

'Yes.'

'Did you try to bring me here?'

'Yes. That's what the spell was for.'

'So it worked?'

'Must have. You're here, aren't you?'

'I suppose I am. I'm certainly not at home with Mum taking a photo of me.'

A slow smile spread across Denzil's face. 'Welcome to Northwood Village,' he said.

hanks for inviting me,' said Sam.

'Sorry I couldn't call you first,' said Denzil. 'We're a bit slow getting phones here.'

Sam wasn't listening. She was staring at the corner of the house, her eyes wide with astonishment. A woman stood there, with a fat white goose struggling in her arms. She wore a long, rough brown dress and a white apron. She too wore headgear that covered her shoulders, though hers was made of softer material and embroidered on the edges. Her stockings were wrinkled about her ankles, and were knitted in stripes of black and orange wool. Her cheeks were bright red with the cold, and her hands, as they held the straining goose, were shaking.

'Mother Goodhart,' stammered Denzil. 'Oh, blimey.'

Mother Goodhart dropped the goose and slowly sank to the ground.

'Good Lord preserve us,' she said, in hushed and prayerful tones. She bowed low, covering her face with her apron. 'An angel has visited our village.'

Sam started to giggle.

Denzil bit his lower lip, and wondered whether he should make a forgetting-spell for Mother Goodhart.

But before he could remember it, Mother Goodhart slowly stood up, her hands clasped in joy and adoration. She looked one last time on the angel's face, then fled after the escaped goose, to tell all of Northwood about the heavenly visitation.

'Well,' said the angel to Denzil, 'are you going to give me some clothes to warm me up, or do I have to stand out here and do aerobics?'

Margaret Mahy

THE MAN WHOSE MOTHER WAS A PIRATE

ILLUSTRATED BY MARGARET CHAMBERLAIN

There was once a little man who had never seen the sea, although his mother was an old pirate woman. The two of them lived in a great city far, far from the seashore.

The little man always wore a respectable brown suit and respectable brown shoes. He worked in a neat office, and wrote down rows of figures in books, ruling lines under them.

Well, one day his mother said, 'Shipmate, I want to see the sea again.

I want to fire my old silver pistol, and see the waves jump with surprise.'

'Oh, Mother!' said the little man. 'We haven't got a car, or a bicycle, or a horse. And we've no money, either. All we have is a wheelbarrow and a kite.'

'We must make do!' his mother answered sharply. 'I will go and load my pistol and polish my cutlass.'

The little man went to work.

'Please, Mr Fat,' he begged his boss, 'please may I have two weeks' holiday to take my mother to the seaside?'

'I don't go to the seaside!' said Mr Fat crossly. 'Why should you?'

'It is for my mother,' the little man explained. 'She used to be a pirate.'

'Oh, well, that's different,' said Mr Fat who rather wished he were a pirate himself. 'But make sure you are back in two weeks, or I will buy a computer.'

So off they set, the little man pushing his mother in the wheelbarrow, and his mother holding the kite. His mother wore a green scarf and gold earrings. Between her lips was her old black pipe, behind one ear a crimson rose. The little man wore his brown suit buttoned, and his brown shoes tied. He trotted along pushing the wheelbarrow.

As they went, his mother talked about the sea. She told him of its voices.

'It sings with a booming voice and smiles as it slaps the ships. It screams or sadly sighs. There are many voices in the sea and a lot of gossip, too. Where are the great whales sailing? Is the ice moving in Hudson Bay? What is the weather in Tierra del Fuego? The sea knows the answers to a lot of questions, and one wave tells another.'

'Oh yes, Mother,' said the little man whose shoes hurt him rather.

'Where are you off to?' asked a farmer.

'I'm taking my mother to the seaside,' said the little man. 'I wouldn't go there myself,' said the farmer. 'It's up and down with the waves, in and out with the tide. The sea doesn't stay put the way a good hill does.' 'My mother likes things that don't stay put,' said the little man.

Something began to sing in the back of his mind. 'Could that be the song of the sea?' he wondered, as he pushed the wheelbarrow. His mother rested her chin on her knees.

'Yes, it's blue in the sunshine,' she said, 'and it's grey in the rain. I've seen it golden with sunlight, silver with moonlight and black as ink at night. It's never the same twice.'

They came to a river. There was no boat. The little man tied the wheelbarrow to the kite. A wind blew by, ruffling his collar, teasing his neat moustache. 'Hold tight, Mother!' he called.

Up in the air they went as the wind took the kite. The little man dangled from the kite string. His mother swung in her wheelbarrow-basket. 'This is all very well, Sam,' she shouted to him. 'But the sea – ah, the sea! It tosses you up and pulls you down. It speeds you along, it holds you still. It storms you and calms you. There's a bit of everything in the sea.'

'Yes, Mother,' the little man said. The singing in the back of his mind was growing louder and louder. As he dangled from the kite string the white wings of the birds in the sky began to look like the white wings of ships at sea.

The kite let them down gently on the other side of the river.

'Where are you going?' asked a philosopher fellow who sat reading under a tree.

'I'm taking my mother to the sea,' said the little man.

'What misery!' cried the philosopher.

'Well, I didn't much like the idea to start with,' said the little man, 'but now there's this song in the back of my mind. I'm beginning to think I might like the sea when I get there.'

'Go back, go back, little man,' cried the philosopher.

'The wonderful things are never as wonderful as you hope they'll be. The sea is less warm, the joke less funny, the taste is never as good as the smell.'

'Hurry up! The sea is calling,' shouted the pirate mother, waving her cutlass from the wheelbarrow. The little man trundled his mother away, and as he ran he noticed that his brown suit had lost all its buttons.

Then something new came into the wind's scent. 'Glory! Glory! There's the salt!' cried his mother triumphantly.

Suddenly they came over the hill.

Suddenly there was the sea.

The little man could only stare. He hadn't dreamed of the BIGNESS of the sea. He hadn't dreamed of the blueness of it. He hadn't thought it would roll like kettledrums, and swish itself on to the beach. He opened his mouth, and the drift and the dream of it, the weave and the wave of it, the fume and foam of it never left him again. At his feet the sea stroked the sand with soft little paws. Farther out, the great, graceful breakers moved like kings into court, trailing the peacock-patterned sea behind them.

The little man and his pirate mother danced hippy-hoppy-happy hornpipes up and down the beach. The little man's clothes blew about in the wind, delighted to be free at last.

A rosy sea captain stopped to watch them. 'Well, here are two likely people,' he cried. 'Will you be my bo'sun, Madam? And you, little man, you can be my cabin boy.'

'Thank you!' said the little man.

'Say, "Aye, aye, sir!"' roared the captain.

'Aye, aye, sir!' replied the little man just as smartly as if he'd been saying, 'Aye, aye, sir!' all his life.

MARGARET MAHY

So Sailor Sam went on board with his pirate mother and the sea captain, and a year later someone brought Mr Fat a green glass bottle with a letter in it. 'Having a wonderful time,' the letter read. 'Why don't you run off to sea, too?'

And if you want any more moral to the story than this, you must go to sea and find it.

Pauline Cartwright

KAHUKURA AND THE SEA FAIRIES

ILLUSTRATED BY TE MAARI GARDINER

The Maori had always made fish-hooks of bone, curved and sharp so no fish that took one could spit it out. They had always made spears, barbed so that when one was thrust downwards there would be no escape for any sea creature beneath.

By these means they caught fish – but only one at a time. Until Kahukura learnt a special secret . . .

Kahukura was a young Maori chief. He had pale hair and light skin, but it was not just this that made him different from other chiefs. It was his dreams.

'He is always staring out to sea as though he searches for something,' said one old man to another. They looked at the young man, sitting alone, distant from his people. 'Dreaming, always dreaming,' the other answered.

'Perhaps,' suggested one very old man, 'he searches for the spirit path that leads to the last pohutukawa in this land?' 'No, he is too young to be thinking of death,' said the first. 'I don't know what it is he searches for . . .'

Kahukura never told anyone that what he searched for was the secret of an unfinished dream.

The dream had come to him on many nights. It was always of the same place – a distant Northland beach where music played and lights danced on the waters of the bay. In his dream, Kahukura crept over the sand towards the lights. Always, before he could get close enough to see what they were, the young chief would wake up and the dancing lights would vanish into the cloak of darkness that was night.

'There is a secret in the ending of my dream,' he would say to himself. 'If only I knew it, I would have something special to give to my people.'

So he would sit and stare northwards, narrowing his eyes against the glint of the coastal waters, as if he might suddenly see the ending of his dream. Then the dream stopped coming. But the power of it stayed with the young chief. He could still see the curve of the cliffs, the sweep of the bay. Kahukura decided he should travel north to seek out its secret. He gathered his tribe and told them he would be gone for some time as he was seeking something special that he would bring back for them.

'Wait for me,' he said. 'Watch, and wait for my return.'

Kahukura set out alone on the long journey far to the north.

He walked through the forests of Tane. He strode along the edges of the waters of Tangaroa. Sometimes he moved in the warmth of the daytime and sometimes in the shadows of the night. But always he followed the path that he had trodden before in his dream.

Late one evening he was drawn by the distant sound of music. He quickened his footsteps and moved around a jutting cliff. Beyond lay the curve of a bay. Kahukura knew it at once. This was the place – the beach on which he had walked in his dream. He stepped onto the soft white sand and crouched behind a rock to await the full darkness of night.

When darkness came, the music grew louder. Peering over the rock, Kahukura saw the dancing lights of his dream and realised that they were made by torches. The torches were held by people in canoes, gliding into the bay. There was a soft splashing of paddles. Kahukura straightened, still hidden, he knew, by the darkness of the night. He peered at the canoes and the dancing lights. His heart thudded with excitement. He was close to finding out the secret of his dream.

The canoes seemed to be linked in twos by curving lines that dragged between them. Within the curves, the waters of the sea bubbled and splashed as if there were many fish contained inside them. Kahukura watched as the canoes were beached and the fishermen jumped out.

'Pull up the net,' they called. 'Pull up the net!'

Kahukura, who did not understand the word 'net', moved closer. He saw the fishermen tug on ropes. Out of the water they drew a mass of flax strings, tied like a spider's web in a spreading pattern. In the flax strings were many, many fish. Not one fish as on a hook; not one fish as on a spear; but hundreds of fish.

Kahukura was amazed. This was magic. He stared at the fisher people under the light of their torches. Their hair was fair and their skin was pale. These were no ordinary fishermen. They were fairies from the sea! The pile of fish grew huge and silver as the fairies plucked their catch from the nets. Kahukura thought of how having such nets would improve the life of his people. Having found the secret of his dream, he knew he must now find a way to take one of the nets home.

Glancing at the sand, Kahukura saw that the sea fairies left not even footprints as they worked. He knew that they would not leave a net unless he could think of a way to trick them into doing so.

He edged further out onto the sand. Not a single fairy looked at him, for, like them, his hair was fair, his skin pale. Boldly he walked towards them, mingled with them. Not one noticed that he was a mortal.

Kahukura saw that they were threading the fish onto flax strings. The young chief smiled to himself and set to helping them.

He picked up a flaxen cord, but did not tie a knot in the end before he began threading it with fish. The fish fell off, and a fairy came to help him.

Kahukura began to thread another cord without a knot. Another fairy came back from the canoe where he had loaded his fish to help Kahukura tie the fish on firmly.

Over and over again, Kahukura threaded fish onto lines that he knew would not hold them. Over and over again, the fairies, not realising that he was not one of them, came to help. Now and again Kahukura glanced at the horizon.

Suddenly, he saw what he looked for – the first rays of morning sun. He dropped the cord he was holding and leapt to his feet.

'Look out!' he cried to the fairies around him and to those still bundling up the nets to load into the canoes. 'Here comes the sun!'

Some of the sea fairies grabbed their nets. Some dashed towards the canoes, dangling the rethreaded strings of fish. Some just fled with cries of alarm.

The cries soon faded to nothing for the sun rose fast, stretching out its golden fingers over the fairies. Along with their canoes and everything in them, the fairies vanished.

Such was their haste in trying to escape the morning light that they had left – as Kahukura had hoped they would – a net on the beach.

There were no dancing lights now; no music; no dark water. Kahukura stood alone in the sun-flooded bay holding the magic that he had tricked the sea fairies into leaving behind them.

He had the secret of his dream.

The young chief took the net back to his people and showed them the magic.

Soon, other tribes learnt the way of weaving and patterning flax strings to make nets.

And often, when they had eaten their fill and still had fish left over to dry, they talked of the young chief Kahukura – the man who had gone in search of a dream and who was clever enough to trick the

fairies of the sea so that all Maori came
to know a way of fishing for many, many fish at one time.

Ken Catran

FOCUS AND THE DEATH-RIDE

ILLUSTRATED BY BRIAN HARRISON

*Bryce and Focus are unaware of the terrible
black dangers ahead . . .*

I like to think I am not a coward. I am certainly very cautious
and believe in non-violence because it is quite true that he who
runs away, lives to fight another day. The squeal of that gate and
the horrific gothic metaphor it produced in my mind, made me think
at once about living another day. Of course I made it sound very
casual as though it was the most natural thing in the world to think
of right now.

'Ah, let's come back tomorrow, Focus,' not even adding, when the
sun is shining.

Focus stopped and looked at me. She scratched her hair, then rubbed
black hands down her black face and gave a loud sigh in the

darkness. 'Okay, Bryce, quite right,' she said, 'yeah, go.'

I was mind-zapped! Focus admitting someone else was right! I tried to be forgiving and understanding in victory and also, of course, to sound just as casual. 'Mr Trang's place'll still be open,' I said. 'The shakes are on me.' And fool that I was, I was halfway back to the bikes before realising that Focus wasn't behind me. The feeling that she had once again got the better of me clutched my body like a giant crab, but I just turned very slowly and  sauntered back up. I even remembered to hook my thumbs in my belt.

'Focus, time to quit.'

'You quit, Bryce,' she said and then grinned, her white teeth flashing in the moonlight. 'I'm going to tell Percy he's got friends and to stop being silly.'

'I suppose you expect me to come with you,' I said, thinking of about a million reasons why not, that I could have blasted off like missiles as we walked down the path together.

'I wouldn't dream of forcing you,' she said calmly.

I nearly asked bitterly, so how come we are nearly at the door? But there was a chance Percy's dog would hear us. Not that it mattered because a moment later, Focus – without a single thought for our safety – called out loudly, 'Mr McAllister, are you in there?'

No answer. There was a small light on in the hall, enough to outline all those dark propeller blades spread like dinosaur bones on the walls. The dank, unhappy smell of the house crept out around us like a waiting silence and Focus called again.

'Mr McAllister, we talked to Mr Klein. We know you have some problems.' Her voice shook just a tiny bit and our hands grabbed tight. 'We would like to help.'

'Corr – iidd – orrr ennndd . . .'

The ghastly whisper came creeping around us like cold fingers from a black unknown. It was distorted and sagging as though someone was stretching inhuman vocal cords and in the same moment, a red light came on at the end of the hall. It was like a single evil eye looking at us, daring us to come closer. As Focus asked, I had put all my gothic fantasies on the backburner, but now they were flooding up into molten life. And that evil red light winked like the crafty eye of a devil, enticing us in.

'Sounds like Percy wants to talk to us,' Focus said in the same calm tone that now did not fool me in the slightest.

'I think he's just trying to scare the hell out of us,' I whispered back.

'Eee-nnnddd . . .' whispered the saggy inhuman voice, all around us like stereo from the grave and ahead, the devil-eye winked again as though beckoning us forward.

'Sure he is,' said Focus. 'But he also left the door open.'

We were in the corridor now. The door leading to the lounge was shut and only the hall-light and that awful red glare ahead showed us the way. I felt now a little bit the way Focus did. That we had come this far and we had to see it to the end, that we had already stepped across the black fringes of Percy's nightmare.

The red light outlined a doorway. I hadn't seen it the last time I was in the house, because even with the light it was set into the wall and looked new and modern. Beside it was a small inset digital unit that suddenly winked numbers and the door opened.

'Electronic lock,' whispered Focus. 'Shall we go in?'

This sort of question was typical of Focus. A lock that opened automatically was obviously being controlled from somewhere else by Percy's skinny brown hand, and it was obviously meant to entice us in. I nearly yelled NO, but suddenly, strangely, I was feeling the way Focus did, like an explorer on the edge of an unknown ocean.

So Focus – expecting me to refuse but go along anyway, pulled by the force of her personality – looked at me with a sudden pleased astonishment when I whispered, 'Yes'.

'Way to go, Bryce,' she said and pushed the door open before I could do the sensible thing and change my mind.

We were facing one side of a narrow, dark-painted tubular corridor. It went in either direction and one side ended in a perspex bubble, a seat and two twin-barrelled guns pointing out. *That* should have told me, but it didn't, not until Focus nudged me and pointed at the other end. There was a flickering darkness, made up of tiny outlines of light. And there was a gathering and vibrating sound underfoot.

We walked down the tube-corridor to the other end. We went up a step and past a little desk and a radio transmitter. And even without looking back, I knew that the entrance was closed in darkness. And I had this awful been-here-before feeling as though parts of an icy cold jigsaw were slotting themselves around me as we went forward into another curved perspex dome that bulged out ahead. In one of the seats sat a leather-clad figure, the helmeted head turned from us. And at the same time, the thundering-vibrating sound gathered underfoot. Beside me, Focus gasped aloud the very thoughts in my mind.

'Bryce!' she said in a whisper that screamed. 'This is the flight-deck of a Lancaster bomber!' And as she spoke, we heard that stabbing-distorted whisper boom around us and the vibrating sound grew like thunder.

As it did, the brown-leather figure seemed to jerk and it turned its head with a horrible bone-clicking sound that made itself heard over the growing thunder. Gloved hands were jiggling over the controls while the roaring noise grew louder and the seated thing turned its face towards us.

It was a skull, grinning bony and fleshless with a horrible white-toothed smile as though pleased to be risen from the grave. And as it clack-tooth grinned at us, the thundering noise grew louder and lights sped past outside as everything gathered speed around us. Now there was a loud roaring noise like the black throat of hell opening, and Focus yelled, this time out very loud as the floor slanted suddenly upwards.

'Bryce, it's taking off!'

I freaked and I have to admit this; I am not afraid to admit it because Focus freaked too. As the growl-thunder of engines started and the floor steepened, we didn't stop to think if we had trespassed more than fifty years backwards or whether all this was a Percy-generated hi-tech nightmare. So I turned at the same moment Focus did and we both ran down the tubular walkway towards the entrance.

I had never realised how good a runner Focus was. I have always been very good myself and was ahead of her out of the entrance and back into the corridor. Outside, though, she caught up with me as we headed down the drive and we vaulted over the gate like a pair of Siamese twins joined at the hip. We tumbled down into the hedge and behind us the noise stopped with a thin high sound that might have been Percy's laughter or the gate to hell slamming shut.

Tessa Duder

NIGHT RACE TO KAWAU

ILLUSTRATED BY KEGGIE CAREW
LINE DRAWINGS BY JANINE BROUGHAM

*Sam tries not to panic when her thrilling
night-time sail becomes a terrifying ordeal.*

After eight! They had been racing over two hours now. The evening sun still shone warmly on the back of Sam's neck as she sat at the tiller. She gave a huge stretch. This was the life. Free of school, of people, all those strange faces, of traffic, Mum in a good mood, the boat taking them to Kawau. Tomorrow, after a lie-in and a swim off the boat before breakfast, they would go looking for wallabies and wekas on the island.

On the dot of half past seven – Jane had seen to that, although how she knew it was half past seven intrigued them all; it was intuition, she said smugly – Mrs Starr dispensed the pavlova with her usual comments about 'sickly stuff, all calories and no taste!' Nonetheless, she served herself a piece and seemed to enjoy it as much as anyone.

That over, the family settled down again to a long silence, Jane and Jeremy reading on the bunks below and Sam and her parents in the cockpit.

The wind seemed to be lighter than ever. Sam became aware of a growing sense of isolation. The world had shrunk; it consisted only of *Aratika* and her crew on a little patch of sea. The other boats were illusions, ghost ships, too far away now to distinguish sail numbers. Some had chosen to keep further to the west, closer to the East Coast beaches and out of the tidal stream; most, like the Starrs, had passed within a few hundred kilometres of the red and white striped Rangitoto lighthouse. They seemed to be holding their own, but Sam knew that the newer, lighter boats would inevitably draw ahead and that from now on it would be difficult to tell how they stood in the race until they sailed past the committee boat in Bon Accord Harbour. Each yacht would follow its own course through the summer night.

Ahead, but mostly astern, the great fleet spread its sails as far as the eye could see. Occasionally glancing behind to check the surface of the water for ruffles of wind, as Dad had taught her to do, Sam could see a throng of tiny spinnakers, round and bright as lollipops. Those would be the Fourth, Third, Second and finally the sleek giants of the First Division. But there were no little puffs sneaking up from behind; the wind seemed to have dropped to a point where Dad was having difficulty in keeping the spinnaker full. *Aratika* was barely making way through the water. All Sam could do, as helmsman, was hold the tiller steady and keep her on course for Tiri passage. Her eyelids were dropping, like the spinnaker.

'The tide is ebbing,' said her father suddenly. He must have seen her head nodding. 'Eight o'clock tide, so it's just past slack water. That will help a bit. It flows through the passage at a fair clip.'

Jerked out of her half-sleep, Sam peered ahead over the top of the upturned dinghy. The fleet would soon thread itself through the narrow passage between the mainland and Tiritiri Island. Already the powerful Tiri light was sending its flash around the sky every fifteen seconds.

Sam felt a sudden chill as she watched the final sliver of sun disappear behind the western ranges. The sea, although calm enough, had lost its friendliness and was now a sinister molten grey, streaked with lemon and pink. Her small world seemed even smaller. She became very conscious of her father's strength. At home, Mum might be the pivot around which the household revolved, but on the boat Dad was the skipper, who had the last word. She felt she could face anything, the wildest storm, the most magnificent waves, as long as Dad was in charge.

She shivered. 'Can I go and get a jumper, Mum?'

'It's all right. I'll get them, Sam. We're all going to need one soon.' Mrs Starr disappeared into the now murky cabin below.

'Jeremy seems to be fast asleep,' came the low voice. 'That's good,' said Mr Starr. 'Give him a chance to rest that head. Hopefully, he'll sleep right through the night. Tuck him up well, Mum. What's Jane doing? Asleep too?' 'Reading with her pocket torch. Not doing her eyes any good,' said Mrs Starr, reappearing at the hatchway with an armful of jumpers. 'Don't you think we'd better get that spinnaker down, Nick? It'll be dark in about fifteen minutes, maybe less.'

'Won't we get left behind?' asked Sam. 'We'll be the only boat in the fleet without a spinnaker. Can't we take it down later?' Her father sighed. 'I think your mother's right, Sam. If we'd had Terry we'd have been able to carry it right through to Kawau. Pity. But we won't do too badly under the main and big jenny, you'll see.' He temporarily cleated the spinnaker sheet, stood up on the after deck and yawned noisily.

Sam looked sadly up at the big sail and then at the rest of the fleet. All around them red, white and green lights were appearing like glow-worms against the darkening sea.

'Can you put the navigation lights on before you come up, Mum?' Dad said, both arms raised to the sky in a prolonged stretch. 'I hope . . .'

He stopped abruptly, squinting at the leading boats now passing through the Tiri passage.

'What on earth . . .?'

Sam, alerted, looked up at her father's large shape outlined against the pale lemon sky. He was now pulling on his jumper with a purposeful air.

'What is it, Dad?'

'I should have noticed this earlier. You wouldn't believe it! Those boats ahead have picked up quite a northerly. Look at them, hard on the wind. God knows where it's come from!'

'A northerly? There was nothing in the forecast about northerlies.' Mrs Starr sounded peevish. She liked things to be orderly and predictable.

The tiny sails of the Sixth Division a couple of kilometres ahead were unmistakably heeled to a northerly. Sam knew what that meant: a long beat all the way to Kawau and hardly the quiet race they had expected.

'We've less than five minutes to get the spinnaker down before we catch that wind, Mum,' said Mr Starr, loosening off the spinnaker guy, then swinging himself monkey-fashion along the deck until he disappeared into the half-light. After the long period of inactivity and calm, Sam felt thrown off balance and suddenly uneasy as helmsman.

'You take her, Mum,' she said plaintively.

'Just a minute, Sam.' She called for'ard. 'Nick? Do you want me to

help you with the spinnaker?' She didn't sound too eager about it, thought Sam.

'I could help Dad,' said Sam quickly. Of the two options, she would rather help her father on the foredeck than be in charge of the tiller when the wind changed.

'No thanks,' came a voice from behind the upturned dingy. 'I can operate better on my own. You take the tiller, Mum. You, Sam, be ready to let go the spinnaker guy when I tell you. And get the lifelines out of the port locker, Sam. We might need them later.'

Sam thankfully handed over the tiller and headed below.

'What's going on?' asked Jane sleepily. 'There's a northerly coming,' said Sam, feeling the lifelines neatly coiled in their usual place in the locker. She put them on the floor just at the foot of the steps where they would be easy to find later on. 'We've got to get the spinnaker down. Or rather Dad has.'

'He's making enough noise about it. What's he doing up there?' said Jane as the cabin resounded to three or four heavy thuds and bangs above them. 'Sounds like an elephant.'

'I don't know. That might be the spinnaker pole, I suppose.'

'Sounds like he dropped it.'

'We'd soon know if he did,' said Sam, climbing back into the cockpit.

Her mother was looking anxious, and surprisingly the spinnaker was still up and drawing. Sam had expected to find it down, and Dad busy tidying things up on the foredeck.

'Jane,' Mrs Starr was calling in her best fusspot voice. 'We're going to be tacking. Can you check that Jeremy isn't going to fall out of his bunk? Stuff some cushions under him.' 'I was just going to sleep,' grumbled Jane. 'Weren't we all?' said Mrs Starr tartly. 'Look at that wind on the water, Sam.' Advancing slowly across the leaden sea was a clear line, dark as charcoal, where the wind was ruffling the surface into little short waves. Even as she looked, Sam felt a whisper brush past her cheek and *Aratika* make a slight curtsey to port, the spinnaker restless.

'What's holding up Dad?' said Mrs Starr.

'I don't know.' The spinnaker was still full, but any minute now it would surely collapse, caught aback by the advancing northerly. 'Does he need a torch?'

'It might help. Ask him. There's obviously something he's having to sort out first, although I can't imagine what.' Again the yacht heeled to another puff of wind, this time collapsing the spinnaker and disturbing all the saucepans in the galley below. Sam stood on the cockpit seat and leaned forward over the cabin top. Strangely, there was no movement to be seen anywhere on the foredeck.

'Dad? Do you want a torch?' In the shadows behind the upturned dinghy and the solid wooden mast, it was impossible to see what he was doing. 'Dad! Can I bring you a torch?' she called.

Again there was no response. Sam suddenly realised that there had been no movement on the foredeck since those earlier thuds. Perplexed, she turned and looked at her mother.

'Nick, what's the delay?' shouted Mrs Starr. 'We're going to be caught aback if you don't get that spinnaker down. I'm going to have to run off or something . . .' Just at that moment, a flash from the Tiri light not far away to their right lit up her mother's face. She was standing at the tiller, very tense. Her eyes were wide with fear. Sam knew the same thought had struck them simultaneously.

'Dad,' wailed Sam for'ard into the gloom. Again there was no sound apart from the rustling of the spinnaker as it filled and strained, collapsed and drooped, and filled again. Sam turned back to face her mother.

'He's not there, Mum. He's gone. He's fallen overboard.'

Jack Lasenby

OLD TIP AND THE HOT WATER BOTTLE

ILLUSTRATED BY BOB KERR

'**FROST!**' said Uncle Trev. 'You call this frost?'

I looked at the ice on the windows and thought of the ice on the puddles I'd have to crack with my bare feet on the way to school. There'd be cobwebs sparkling white between the fence wires. The grass blades would be furry with frost. I'd pick a clean piece of ice out of a puddle and chew it. The birds would sit on the telephone lines, fluffed up and too cold to fly. It was my turn to give a talk to the class that morning.

'It is a frost, isn't it?' I asked.

'Of course it's a frost!' said my mother, refilling Uncle Trev's teacup. 'Stop teasing the child. What brings you into Waharoa so early?'

'I came in to buy a hot water bottle,' Uncle Trev said. 'Come out to

the farm and you'll see a real frost.

'It was so cold this morning, Old Tip couldn't bark till I warmed him by the fire. Then he ran down the paddock barking and puffing white breath like a little steam engine.

'I had to wash the cows' bags with warm water before they could let down their milk, and then it froze in the bucket.

'A hawk flew into the shadow of the hill. The frost struck him and he drove into the ground like a frozen spear. I jumped out of his way, stood on a flax bush, and the leaves snapped off like glass breaking.

'I brought my long underpants in off the line, and the legs broke in half as I tried to fold them.

'The pongas down by the river looked like white fountains. Just as the river froze solid, a trout jumped after a fly. When he came down he knocked himself silly on the ice. I cooked him for my breakfast.

'I had to fill the radiator with boiling water and warm the engine with a blowtorch. The crank-handle froze to my hand, and I had to tickle it up with the blowtorch before it would let go.

'As I drove down to the bridge, I thought the engine was backfiring, but it was those big lacebarks exploding as the sap froze in their hearts.'

'Do trees have sap in their hearts?' I asked.

'Course they do, like we have blood in ours.'

'But I thought sap was in the sapwood on a tree.'

My mother smiled grimly. 'The child has a point there.'

'I suppose that's the sort of thing they teach you at school these days,' said Uncle Trev. 'Folks might have dry hearts down here in Waharoa, but not out on my farm. The weeping willows' long branches looked like skirts of icicles. When the wind blew, they jingled like bells, and the sun flashed off them.'

'There's not a breath of wind this morning,' Mum said. 'That's why we've got a frost.'

'Out at the farm,' said Uncle Trev, 'we had a blizzard as well. It blew all the frost off the front paddocks and heaped it against the hills. It was so cold, the ears fell off the rabbits and blew away like dead leaves. Their tails fell off and rolled like white marbles.

'A big cloud came into the shadow of the hills and turned solid, frozen hard by the frost. You should have heard it crunch when it banged into the hillside! It was still stuck there when I left home.'

'There's not a cloud in the sky this morning,' Mum said. 'If there were clouds, there'd be no frost.'

'You don't know you're alive down here in Waharoa! I had to call in here for a cup of tea because mine froze as I poured it. I didn't dare cut the butter to put on my toast.'

'Why not?'

'It would have splintered. A piece could have gone in my eye.'

'A pity a splinter didn't get in your tongue,' said my mother.

'The smoke got so cold going up the chimney,' Uncle Trev said, 'it fell down inside again. I had to find the end, drag it outside, and hang it along the fence. It'll warm up and blow away once the sun gets on it.'

'It was cold when I went to bed last night,' I said, 'so Mum gave me the hot water bottle and took it out when she went to bed.'

'My teeth chattered so much I had to put them under my pillow to keep them quiet,' Uncle Trev said. 'My toes rattled like a stick on corrugated iron.'

'Don't you have a hotty?' I asked.

'I let Old Tip have it till I went to bed,' said Uncle Trev. 'When I wanted it he growled and showed his teeth. He thinks he's smart, but I'm going to fix him tonight. I won't fill his bottle, and he can just put up with the cold. I'm going down to the store for a new one now.

'Old Tip!' said Uncle Trev scornfully. 'He thinks he's clever, but he still doesn't know how to get himself a hot water bottle. He can fill it with water all right, but he has trouble getting the top screwed in, and it leaks on him during the night. He's not all that bright, Old Tip.'

When Uncle Trev left, I was going off to school, so I went out with him to say hello to Old Tip who was sitting in the front of the lorry.

'He stayed out here to keep warm from the engine,' said Uncle Trev.

'Mum wouldn't have let him inside her kitchen anyway.'

'Can you see my hot water bottle underneath him? Don't go trying to lift him up, or he'll take a piece out of your hand! He'll think you're going to take it away.'

I couldn't see the hot water bottle under Old Tip. He stuck his head out the window and wagged his tail as I scratched behind his ears. I hoped Uncle Trev would feel sorry for him and fill his hot water bottle that night.

As I went down the road to school, the ice in the puddles cracked under my bare feet like glass. Mr Jones would have made cocoa for the bus kids. They had to have it because the wind blew through the canvas sides on the school bus, and they froze. I was going to tell the class about the great frost out on Uncle Trev's farm and about Old Tip and his hot water bottle.

Laura Ranger

SANDS

My skin is as smooth
as polished wood.
When my mother strokes me
she sands me·
with her hands.

My skin is as smooth
as a piece of driftwood
on Otaki beach.
Waves smashing,
and sand makes it smooth
as seagull feathers.

Lynley Dodd

THE SMALLEST TURTLE

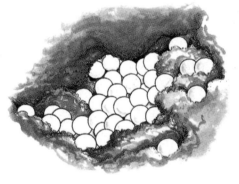

Deep in a safe dark hole
under the sand
lay a nest of turtle eggs.

One day,
they began to hatch.
Soon there were dozens of baby turtles
all wriggling together up through the sand and away.

Except the smallest turtle.

He was late.
All by himself
he scrambled and scrabbled
up, up, up . . .

and out into the shimmery sun.
He blinked at the brightness
and inside his head he heard strange words,
'To the sea – to the sea.'

So away he went,
skitterscatter,
over a shiny grey rock
and past a big black beetle,
around a tree with twisty roots,
down a gravelly hole
and up the other side,
where a sleepy lizard was dozing in the sun,
through some prickly grass
where a spider was weaving a web
and all the time, his head said, 'To the sea – to the sea.'

The sun was burning down
on the smallest turtle.
It made him too hot
and it muddled the words in his head.
He began to go round and round
in circles.

He crept into the shade
of a big green leaf
to cool down
and as he cooled,
the words in his head
slowly came back again,
'To the sea – to the sea.'

So on and on went the smallest turtle
until at last he stopped to rest.
He was getting very tired.
Suddenly he heard something.
It was the sound of waves
crashing and hissing on the sand.
The words in his head became stronger than ever,
'To the SEA – to the SEA.'

But there was danger.
Gulls were wheeling and whirling
up in the sky, looking with beady greedy eyes
for a baby turtle lunch.

The smallest turtle didn't wait.

Down the scorching sand he scrabbled and skittered,
    faster, faster,
        away from the gulls,
            past the crabs,
                over the seaweed,
                    over the shells,
                        over the stones and . . . .

at last he felt cool cool water
on his hot tired sandy body.
And as he swam down,
down,
down,
he knew.
'It's the SEA,' he sang, 'it's the SEA!'

Joy Cowley

TULEVAI
AND THE SEA

ILLUSTRATED BY
MANU SMITH

E

very morning Tulevai went fishing.
Every morning he took fish home to his mother.

The sea watched him. 'Ah,' said the sea. 'What a strong boy he is. How well he throws that fishing spear. I think I will make him my slave.'

So the sea called in a voice as sweet as honey, 'Tulevai, Tulevai, jump out of your canoe. You can look after my fish in their sea of coral.'

But Tulevai
did not listen.

So the sea called again, in a voice as soft as a flower, 'Tulevai, Tulevai, jump out of your canoe. You can make me a house of yellow shells.'

But Tulevai did not listen.

The sea became angry and went to the wind. 'Wind, wind, help me to catch Tulevai.'
'What will you give me?' asked the wind, who was always greedy.
'A necklace of foam,' said the sea.
'That is not enough,' said the wind.
'And you can have the sails of ships, the feathers of a white bird, and a dead whale,' said the sea.

The wind was satisfied.
It took a deep breath.
Then it blew and blew.

The water heaped up in enormous waves. Tulevai's canoe tipped over, and he sank to the bottom of the sea.

When Tulevai failed to come home, his mother looked for him up and down the beach. All she found was his canoe washed up on the sand.

'Drowned,' whispered the palm trees.
'He has not drowned,' said Tulevai's mother.
'Sharks!' screeched the seagulls.
'He has not been eaten by sharks,' she said.
'The sea took him, and I am going to get him back.'

She went to the wind. 'Wind, Wind, please help me
get Tulevai back from the sea.'
'What will you give me?' asked the greedy wind.
'A necklace of smoke from my cooking fire,' she said.
'That is not enough.' said the wind.
'But it is all I have,' she said.
'Then I cannot help you,' said the wind.
'Then I will get him back myself,' said Tulevai's mother.
She went to the edge of the sea and pushed.

The sea laughed out loud. It called, 'What are you doing,
you silly woman?'
'I want my son, Tulevai,' she said.
'You cannot have him,' said the sea.
'I will push you out of the way and I will find him,' she said.
'Push all you like,' laughed the sea. 'You will never move me.
I am too big. I cover half the world.'
'My love is bigger,' said the woman, and she went on pushing.

'I am too strong,' said the sea, 'I am as strong as a thousand mountains.'

'My love is stronger,' Tulevai's mother said, and she picked up the edge of the sea like a mat and slowly rolled it back from the beach.

The sea tried to fight her. 'Stop!' it cried.

'Give me my son!' demanded Tulevai's mother.

'Never!' roared the sea.

'Then I will go on pushing,' she said.

And she did. Back went the sea in a giant roll. Back from the coral and the starfish. Back from the wrecks of sunken boats. Back from the monsters who lived in the mud . . .

And still Tulevai's mother went on pushing.

At last she found her son. He was sitting in a forest of coral, crying for his home. 'Tulevai!' she cried. The boy jumped up.

'Mother!
Mother!'

'Run,
Tulevai!' she said.
'Run as fast as you can!'

Tulevai ran towards the beach, past the monsters, past the caves and past the boats. He ran over the wet coral, over the shells and starfish. He ran through the palm trees.

When he was safe, his mother unrolled the sea again. 'I told you I would get him back,' she said to the sea.

The sea did not answer.

Today, the sea still hunts for Tulevai. Twice a month, when the moon is new and when the moon is full, the sea looks for him. Right up the beach it comes, calling in a voice as sweet as honey,
       'Tulevai, Tulevai, Tulevai . . .'

Joyce West

DROVERS ROAD

ILLUSTRATED BY JOYCE WEST

Bugle finds a home.

All the stray animals that come to Drovers Road seem to stay here. Not that I blame them for that.

The place is always more or less overrun with dogs. My Uncle Dunsany has half a dozen working dogs of his own, and the shepherds all have their own dogs, and there are always a litter or two of puppies coming on, and someone is sure to have a couple of pig-dogs for hunting at the weekends. Some of Dunsany's dogs have won cups at trials, but none of them is quite like our Bugle.

In fact I don't suppose there is another dog anywhere that looks just like Bugle. In colour he is a lovely cream, like one of the hounds you see in old-fashioned tapestry. But he is very big, as big as a great dane, and his ears are like a foxhound's, and his stern waves the same way, but he has a huge neck and throat like a bull-mastiff's, and his jowls hang down like a bloodhound's. He looks so frightfully fierce that people have been known to come to the gate and go away hurriedly at the sight of him lying asleep in the sun. (As a matter of fact Bugle is almost too kind-hearted to snap at a fly, and Dunsany says that if a burglar came into the house Bugle would make him a cup of tea.)

We were coming back from Renny's Crossing one day, the two boys and I, and we turned round and saw this huge, peculiar-looking thing limping along at our horses' heels. He was so thin that his bones nearly stuck through his skin, and he was filthy, and one ear was torn and bleeding.

Hugh got down and called him, and he came slinking slowly up, wriggling on his stomach in the dust, taking about five minutes to get close enough for Hugh to touch him. Hugh talked to him and patted him for a while before he even tried to look at the injured paw. Hugh is very good with animals, and he is wonderful at helping them when they are hurt; that is what made him first think of being a doctor. When he turned the dog's paw he saw that there was a thorn driven deeply into the soft pad.

'It's a big one,' he said, 'and buried deep. Has any one got a pin?'

'I've got one in the belt of my jodhpurs,' I said.

Aunt Belle was always very angry if we used safety-pins where we should have had buttons, but I had managed to get away that morning without her noticing it, which was convenient for Bugle.

I gave the safety-pin to Hugh; fortunately it was a small sharp one. I helped to hold Bugle's paw steady while Hugh dug. By this time Bugle had decided not to be frightened any more; he licked our hands all the time we were trying to get the thorn out.

'There!' said Hugh at last, and Bugle stopped lying on his back and got up and walked a few steps on his injured paw, trying it out. He decided that it did not hurt him, and came bounding back and lay down at our feet looking as pleased as if someone had left him a fortune.

'Bet you he follows us home now,' said Merry. 'Dunsany will be wild.' 'Well, he really should have some disinfectant put on that foot of his,' said Hugh. 'I think he should have some disinfectant put all over him,' I said. 'Go away!' said Hugh half-heartedly. 'Shoo! Shoo! Go home, dog!' said Merry, even more weakly.

Bugle grinned and waved his stern so violently that he almost upset himself. Then he followed our horses down into the river. The water was fairly deep that day and he had to swim for it, and he landed fifty yards downstream from us. We thought that we had shaken him off, but he came galloping over the stones after us, shedding streams of water at every bound, but still as dirty as ever.

Dunsany was sitting on the back porch mending a bridle when we got home. Bugle had followed us to the stables while we unsaddled the horses, and followed us up to the house again, and squeezed through the fence after us, and there he was coming up the back path at our heels.

'Land sakes!' said Aunt Belle, appearing in the back doorway. 'Is that a dog?' 'It looks a bit like one,' said Dunsany, 'but I think it's something they've dug up out of the churchyard.'

Bugle sank lower on his legs, and waved himself violently from side to side, and grinned apologetically in Dunsany's face. At which Jasper, Dunsany's big kelpie, rose up from lying on the veranda behind him and growled.

Bugle also growled. His lips curled away from huge teeth, and all the dirty hairs on the back of his thin scrawny neck rose up like pigs' bristles. He scraped his paws on the concrete, stiff-legged, and faced up as Jasper, the best fighter at Drovers Road, came prancing down the steps.

It was the best thing he could have done, for Dunsany admires courage very much, either in people or animals.

'Well, he's game, I'll admit that,' he said. 'Sit down, Jasper!'

Jasper looked around at Dunsany and came back slowly and sat down on his master's right hand. Bugle immediately walked up the steps on Dunsany's other hand, and lay down upon the veranda with the air of a dog who has come home. He was so thin that he sounded like a sackful of sticks dropping down upon the boards.

'I thought that you were told you were not to bring any more stray dogs around here!' said Dunsany crossly.

' I'll put some disinfectant on his foot,' said Hugh, 'and then I think we ought to wash him.'

Merry helped to drag round the big wooden tub, and we filled it with warm water and lifted Bugle in. He stood stiffly there, with his head on the edge of the tub and an expression of misery on his face, and we soaped him all over and rubbed him with our hands, and then brought clean water and rinsed him. By then he had gone so stiff with unhappiness that he would not move and we had to lift him out of the tub.

'If that doesn't make him go back where he belongs nothing will!' said Dunsany unkindly, 'and don't you give him anything but a little warm milk to drink or you'll have him sick. He's starved.'

Aunt Belle gave us some clean old rags and we rubbed Bugle dry, and then gave him the warm milk to drink, and he climbed up on to the veranda again and closed his eyes and went to sleep.

'I never knew he was that colour,' said Merry. 'It's pretty.'

My Uncle Dunsany gave a hoot of laughter.

'He might be all right after pigs,' he admitted, 'but I'm not going to have any useless mongrels knocking about the place. He'll have to make himself useful or go in the river with a stone round his neck.'

Neither Hugh nor Merry nor I was very worried because Dunsany had been saying the same thing ever since we could remember, and no dog had ever gone into the river with a stone or anything else round his neck but had lived on at Drovers Road until he died of accident or old age. I remember myself about a dozen; there was Terry, a fox-terrier who chased the hens and never caught any rats, and Flossie, a little half-bred Pekinese that somebody had abandoned on the road, and Red, a beautiful Irish setter who bolted half a mile when he heard a gun shot. They were all quite useless, and more like them.

'What shall we call him?' said Hugh.

'Creamy?' said Merry.

'Creamy!' jeered Hugh. 'It sounds just like a Jersey cow!'

'Biscuit,' I said, and Dunsany guffawed.

'What about Bones?' he said.

'No, he looks like a hound,' said Hugh firmly. 'He must have a hound name like Ranter and Ringwood, Bellman and True. What are some more?'

'Joyful. Venus,' said Merry.

'Bugle,' I said.

At that moment somebody rode up to the gate, and Jasper the Kelpie, sitting by Dunsany, growled. Immediately Bugle, on his other hand, leaped upright, stared around, and then, tilting his head up, brought forth from deep down in his chest a terrific hound bay that shook the windows.

'That settles it,' said Dunsany, when we had recovered from the shock. 'He's Bugle.'

Alistair Te Ariki Campbell

HAIKU

ILLUSTRATED BY BOB BROCKIE

Listlessly on a bare bough
a cicada scrapes
with his bow a few dry notes.

Maurice Duggan

FALTER TOM AND THE WATER BOY

ILLUSTRATED BY GWENDA TURNER

Nobody knew the sea like Falter Tom, except the water boy who appeared one day at half-tide. His skin was as green as a leaf, his hair the colour of copper and he played in the waves like a dolphin . . .

Falter Tom sank into the sea, breathing steadily, his eyes tightly closed. He bumped lightly on the sandy bottom, opened his eyes, and sat up. The first thing he saw was the water boy. The boy's skin was different, the green darker, shot with flecks and speckles of colour, as beautiful as anything Falter Tom had ever seen. The boy's copper-coloured hair stirred in the water as he moved. He brought his strange handsome face very close to the whiskers of Falter Tom.

'There,' the water boy said. 'It's done. You are safe under the sea.
Are you comfortable?'

Falter Tom nodded and began to speak: a cloud of bubbles burst
from his mouth. He tried again and still couldn't get out a word. The
chain of bubbles rose above him. He was very puzzled.

'Don't worry,' the water boy said. 'I'll show you. You must say only
one word with each breath to begin with. Say a word; say it softly.'

'Hallo,' Falter Tom said, very carefully, and was pleased to hear his
own voice again. A tiny string of bubbles went out with the word.
'Hallo,' he said again.

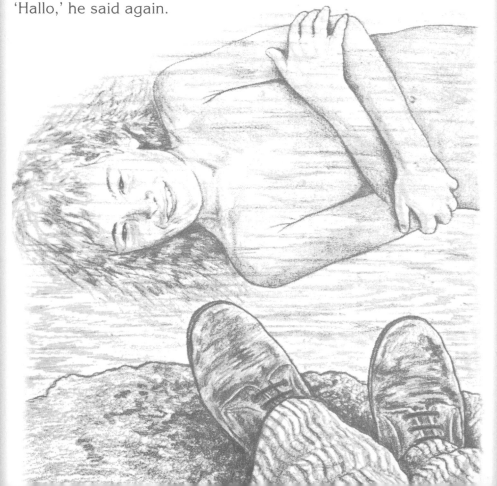

'Splendid,' the boy said. 'In a moment you will have the trick of it. We must rest here a little while, until you get your sea-breath. There's no hurry. We have all the time in the world.'

A cloud of bubbles rose from Falter Tom. The boy smiled and Falter Tom began again.

'It's more like a dream,' Falter Tom said slowly. 'My voice sounds different, quieter; and the sound of it doesn't carry.'

'You can't speak loudly,' the boy said. 'There are no big voices in the sea. They say that if you try to shout the big bubbles take the word up to the surface, and when they break they let free a shout, on the sea top, where there are none to hear. Are you happy?'

'Perfectly,' Falter Tom said. 'Perfectly,' he said again, and watched the bubbles rising. Would there be, he wondered, a tiny echo of the word, muttering over the water when the bubbles broke?

'We must go before the tide turns,' said the boy. 'Low water would uncover us here. Do you feel the stillness? It is dead water, the moment between the tides. It will turn soon. There; do you feel it? The tide is going back. We must go farther out. You'll have to crouch a little at first or your head will poke out.'

Falter Tom stood up, crouching, and walked after the green boy. After a time he stood upright and strolled along, walking on the sloping floor of the sea. Walking was easy, he found. He said a few words to himself, to master the knack of it, then tried a full sentence and a snatch of a song. The song drove the bubbles up in hundreds. Falter Tom smiled; it was very amusing.

The water boy moved on, half swimming, half walking, touching his toes lightly on the sea floor. Falter Tom copied him: it was pleasant to do and not at all difficult; much as if he had been walking on land, with a parachute on his back keeping him almost clear of the ground. They walked so for a little while, and then the water boy stopped and let himself sink until he was sitting down. The sea bottom was no longer sandy, but rocky.

'We must find a place where we can rest,' the water boy said. 'Until you are used to it all you mustn't do too much.'

'I'm fine,' Falter Tom said. 'Never better.'

'I must teach you to swim,' the water boy said. 'It's faster than a sea-walk.'

'Ah,' Falter Tom said. 'There's surely nothing in it if you haven't the worry of keeping afloat.'

He heaved himself forward and swam very slowly and very clumsily around the boy, waving his arms and legs as though he were a crazy windmill feeling the first touch of a fresh wind. The water boy burst out laughing, apologised for being rude, and burst out laughing again. He was so amused that Falter Tom could hardly see him for bubbles.

'We could never get far like that,' the water boy said. 'This is what you do.'

He shot away at a great speed, looking, Falter Tom thought, as though he had been fired from a cannon. His mane of hair streamed behind him. He swam, very fast, in a big loop through the sea, and came back. He circled very slowly around Falter Tom.

'Impossible,' Falter Tom said. 'I'll have to stick to my breast-stroke. That's not something I could manage at all.'

'It's very easy,' the water boy said. 'If you'll only try. The way you do it is this. Imagine you are right up at the very top of the mast, on a ship, and want to dive into the sea.'

'Lad,' Falter Tom said, 'there is nothing one would want less. 'Twould be a way of killing yourself, for sure.'

'Yes, but just imagine,' the water boy said. 'Just pretend. How would you do it, then?'

'Why, I'd dive off,' Falter Tom said. 'Just fall.'

'That's what you have to do, then,' the water boy said. 'You wouldn't try to breast-stroke your way down to the water, would you?'

'Indeed not,' Falter Tom said. 'It would look untidy, and queer.'

'Then if you put your arms straight along your sides and keep your feet together, and keep your balance so that you don't tumble head over heels, you have only to fall through the sea. Up or down, or in whatever direction you like. You use your hands like fins, like a rudder. Do try.'

Falter Tom tried: he kept his feet together and stretched his arms along his sides. He toppled slowly forward, smiling a little, and lay face down, stretched out very stiffly on the bed of the sea.

'You didn't push,' the water boy said.

'I don't remember your mentioning it,' Falter Tom said, in good humour. 'Is it with my feet I'm to push? Or my hands?'

'With your head.'

'Now swither me, boy,' Falter Tom said. 'Am I to stand on my head? A man of my age?'

'Please,' the water boy said. 'I'm serious. It's as if you tried to throw your head away and then dived after it with your body.'

He showed Falter Tom what he meant and Falter Tom tried it. He kept on trying until he could glide forward, rather jerkily, quite a little distance. The boy clapped his hands in delight; it made no sound under the sea. Falter Tom tried again and again, and soon he was able to swim straight ahead, very smoothly and very fast. He was very proud of himself. He had a little trouble turning to come back and lost control and sank down through the sea like a leaf.

'That's where you use your hands,' the water boy said, swimming up to him. 'Follow me; you'll see then.'

They glided off like strong, quick fish, and Falter Tom copied the water boy. They swam a long way, curving and turning, looping and sporting in the pale green light until Falter Tom had learned it all, the long rush, the sweeping turn, the climb, and the dive. Sometimes, however, starting off from the rocky sea floor, he forgot himself and tried to breast-stroke again, and until he remembered the boy's lesson he got nowhere at all. But soon he had the skill off to perfection. He was as proud as a boy who has learned to ride a bicycle or a lively horse.

'It's wonderful,' the boy said, his slanted eyes shining with delight. 'You are very quick. It's because you know the sea. It's how fish swim: but you know that.'

'Indeed, I didn't,' Falter Tom said. 'Though it's an excellent way of getting about. But now that you mention it I'd not look to see a snapper, say, doing the breast-stroke.'

'Then if you're not too tired we will go somewhere where we can rest,' the water boy said, and they swam off, side by side, out into the deeper water where the undersea light paled as they swam.

Elsie Locke

THE RUNAWAY SETTLERS

ILLUSTRATED BY ANTONY MAITLAND

*The true story of a family who ran
away to New Zealand and became pioneers.*

The owls were beginning to call 'morepork' from the hills when Jack gathered his last armful. Most of the big logs were rotten, but his mother needed good sized pieces for that great fireplace. When he saw a dry branch twice as thick as his arm sticking out from a shrub, Jack pulled.

He might have been hauling on a bell-rope, so quickly came the noise of rumbling and grunting. For the second time that day Jack found himself face to face with a young boar – *the* boar.

Before Jack could retreat, the boar charged. With a bound, catching at an overhead branch with his good arm, Jack swung himself clear,

but there was not enough strength in his other shoulder to haul his body up and he had to let go and race around the tree to climb it from the trunk. He sat astride a branch while his angry enemy scraped and backed about among the leaves below.

Should he call out and bring Bill running to help him? No! Jack wanted to settle accounts himself with this robber who had tried to beat him down. He had heard talk of pig hunting among the shepherds at Cashmere and desperately tried to remember. They used dogs, and he had no dog; but he took out his sheath-knife and felt the point. The flax-cutting had not blunted it.

Very quietly he began to ease himself along the branch until it drooped beneath his weight. The boar backed. Jack slid farther: the boar moved again. Had the beast come forward and raised his head, he could have reached Jack's ankle; but he stood back, waiting his opportunity.

Well then, Jack must be first! He braced himself against a second branch, took a flying leap and landed on top of the boar. Somewhere in the back of his memory he could hear a voice saying: *Take him by the hind leg and turn him over.*

Jack grabbed at the leg and held it tightly. But how was he to turn the boar over, while only his own weight kept the lashing beast under control? Perhaps the boar would get tired first! He held on grimly, grunting like the pig with his own exertion, keeping his left hand on the knife.

Then sharply, suddenly, he rolled off, pulled the boar with him and saw the throat stretched out beneath the snout. He thrust out with all the strength his left arm could muster and drove the point into the skin. The boar gave a violent lurch and kicked him over.

Jack scrambled to his feet and did not wait for more. The pain in his shoulder told him that he would never have the strength to repeat the blow. He ran away from the hideous squealing, back down the slope to the cottage. He must get Bill to come with the axe.

In the glow of the firelight he saw his mother take out the damper she had made for their supper. It was a round of dough shaped like a huge scone, made of flour and salt and water, and cooked on a flat stone among the embers. The damper smelt warm and mellow, but it was poor food after all.

'Grab the axe, Bill, I've caught the robber,' shouted Jack. 'The axe?' said Mrs Phipps, startled.

Jack grinned.

'You'll have pork for dinner
tomorrow,' he said.

Dorothy Butler

WHAT PECULIAR PEOPLE!

ILLUSTRATED BY LYN KRIEGLER

Jeremiah Hall
Was astonishingly small —
A tomcat ate him
Boots and all.

Nicholas McFarge
Was phenomenally large —
He had to sleep
On a seagoing barge.

Clarabella Clout
Was voluminously stout —
She squeezed into a phone box
And couldn't get out.

Isabella Lynn
Was frighteningly thin —
She peered down a drainpipe
And fell right in.

Zachariah Paul
Was spectacularly tall —
He stole the clock
Off the old town hall.

Alexander Snort
Was conveniently short —
He slipped through the turnstile
And didn't get caught.

Wilhemina Wood
Was insufferably good —
She'd have sprouted wings
And a halo, if she could.

Gloriana Gadd
Was abominably bad —
She drove her parents
Stark raving mad.

Ebenezer Booth
Had a head uniquely smooth —
A hen tried to hatch it
And that is the TRUTH!

Alistair McNair
Had profusely growing hair —
They put him in the zoo
Because they thought he was a bear.

What peculiar people!
A foolish lot, I fear . . .
I'm glad that I am ordinary . . .
WHOO . . . OO . . . OOPS!
Oh dear.

Jane Cornish

EMILY'S WONDERFUL PIE

ILLUSTRATED BY SUE HITCHCOCK-PRATT

Emily ordered a pie for her lunch,
all squishy and squashy and mincey to munch,
all flakey and bakey and crispy to crunch.

'It's what I love most in the world for my lunch,'
she sighed, with her eye on the pie.

Along came Liz, with a lick of her lips.
'Can I have a bite of your pie for my lunch,
all squishy and squashy and mincey to munch,
all flakey and bakey and crispy to crunch?
I'll be your best friend if you give me some lunch,'
said Liz, with her eye on the pie.

So Emily said, 'Okay. Just a bite.'

Along came Tom with a rumbling tum.
'Can I have a bite of your pie for my lunch,
all squishy and squashy and mincey to munch,
all flakey and bakey and crispy to crunch?
My dad's forgotten to give me my lunch,'
said Tom, with his eye on the pie.

So Emily said, 'Okay. Just a bite.'

Along came Lou with a longing look.
'Can I have a bite of your pie for my lunch,
all squishy and squashy and mincey to munch,
all flakey and bakey and crispy to crunch?
I don't like the look of what I've got for lunch,'
said Lou, with her eye on the pie.

So Emily said, 'Okay. Just a bite.'

Along came Miss Rose with a ravenous sniff.
'Can it be true I smell pie for lunch,
all squishy and squashy and mincey to munch,
all flakey and bakey and crispy to crunch?
I'll swap you some sprouts for a bite of your lunch,'
said Miss Rose, with her eye on the pie.

So Emily said, 'Okay. Just a bite.'

Emily looked at her wonderful pie,
all nibbled and gnawed at, and poked at and picked,
all guzzled and gobbled and chewed at and licked.
'It's nearly all gone,' she moaned. 'I've been tricked.'

Then Emily said,
'Look! Harriet's got a cream doughnut for lunch . . .'

Diana Noonan

A DOLPHIN
IN THE BAY

COLOUR ILLUSTRATION BY GREGORY ROGERS

*Seb, clumsy and fearful, does something
extraordinary one summer . . .*

Behind a quilt of tumbling grey clouds, the moon fought to
light the beach and the bay. Seb skidded down the dune
track, the sand cold and damp beneath his feet. Far down the beach,
fuzzy specks of light twinkled from the town.

Where was she? Where was she? His breathing was rough. His lips
pressed tightly together in a thin hard line. It was so unfair that he
could see no further into the moonlit water than the first shallow
breaking wave.

'I've missed her!' He said it aloud and at the same time felt his eyes
grow wet. 'I've missed her and it's my fault if the yachtsman's never
found.'

The tune
seemed to
carry far out across
the water, beyond
the breaking
waves . . .

His fist closed tightly around the recorder. It was his only hope. What had Bill Kearny said? 'Maybe you'll have to call her in.' Could it be that the dolphin was waiting for him beyond the breakers, waiting for a signal?

His hands were shaking as he raised the recorder to his lips. He blew three sharp notes, high, then low, then high again, linking them together in one eerie wave, hoping at any moment to hear an answering wail. But there was nothing. Unless it's the dolphin tune she wants, thought Seb, remembering that was what he had been playing at the reef yesterday.

Alone on the beach with the light wind ruffling his rain jacket and his feet sinking into the damp sand, Seb played what little he could remember of the tune. There was something about the arrangement of the notes, especially at night, that linked the music to the sea. The tune seemed to carry far out across the water, beyond the breaking waves, beyond the darkness of the bay and into the open sea.

For five, perhaps ten minutes he waited, repeating the tune over and over. In desperation he waded up to his thighs in the water, played one last time and was ready to return to shore when, finally, he heard her. The call was distant at first, little but a faint wailing, a far-off seagull screech, but it was enough to set Seb's heart racing.

He answered. She called again, closer this time. Minutes later, like some magical creature he had conjured up with a spell, she arrived

– a powerful grey torpedo sweeping in on a breaking wave.

He waited for her to leap, but tonight there was no fantastic display of acrobatics. Tonight, to-ing and fro-ing from shallow to deeper water, she led Seb gradually along the beach in the direction of the reef.

He waded at first, stopping frequently to play to her, to check that she was still there. Each time she responded, sweeping like a shadow into the breaking waves, reassuring him she was near. And when at last he was convinced she meant to stay close, Seb left the water to make faster time, running breathlessly along the sand.

It was the reef that stopped him. Even where the dark rock bridge met the sand, waves slapped across it. At night and with high tide fast approaching, it seemed unfamiliar, frightening. Surely she couldn't expect him to go any further?

Abby had said it was possible to walk across the reef to the seal colony in the next bay, but that was in daylight, at low tide, and even then there were inlets to cross. Now the water would be over his head.

He peered into the waves, listening for the dolphin's call, praying that this was as far as she wanted him to go. But from the water on the other side of the rock bridge, she leapt, not once or twice but again and again. To Seb she was only a blur, but he understood her urgency as she crashed with thunderous bellyflops into the sea.

'I can't. I can't do it.' He said it softly and with a sob caught deep in his throat because now he knew Bill Kearny was right. The dolphin had arrived as he had said she would, and if he cooperated, she would lead him to the yachtsman. He thought of returning for help, but would she lead just anyone? What if she refused to reappear or, worse, if no one believed his unlikely story?

Beyond the bridge of rock, the dolphin's leaping grew more frantic. Seb wanted to block his ears, to run home to safety and lights, to his warm sleeping bag.

It was her ear-piercing wail that stopped him: shrill and strong, but as lonely as the sea wind that had whistled around the house on the night of the storm, it was the dolphin's urgent cry for help. Seb knew that if he ignored it, he would also be ignoring the silent cry of the yachtsman.

He adjusted the close-fitting sports goggles on his head, tucked the recorder into the zip pocket of the rain jacket and cautiously stepped onto the rock bridge. Seb Laurie, blind as a bat, too afraid to go out in a fishing boat, too afraid to swim anywhere but between the carefully marked lanes of the school swimming pool, was about to cross a flooded reef at night – with a dolphin his only guide.

Low waves swished about his calves as gingerly he crossed the short span of rock. He fought the temptation to glance behind at the widening distance between himself and the beach, and concentrated instead on searching for the dolphin. And there she was. As he stood looking down into the choppy water, he saw in the moonlight her hump of head and dorsal fin. She was waiting, and now that he was there and knew he had no choice but to follow, he was less afraid than he had expected.

It was a case of doing things mechanically – one movement at a time. Seb squirmed over the side of the rock shelf, and held on. Instantly she was beside him, brushing his legs, smooth and solid as a length of half-submerged driftwood. He let himself slip further into the water, tasted salt, and, still clinging to the rock, threw an arm across her fleshy back. His heart was pounding, but she seemed so calm. She was waiting for him to let go of the rock, to trust her – and he did.

Astride her wide back, his legs and arms clamped about her, Seb rode the dolphin, wrapped in a web of dream, filled both with fear and hope. She swam high, as if instinctively she knew she must keep his face free of the water. He waited for the rasp of solid rock against his leg, for the other side of the inlet to appear out of the greyness, but she delivered him to it gently, nudging him against it as carefully as a tugboat nudges a giant ship into its berth.

He pulled himself dripping from the water, grazing his knees and hands on the flat tongue of exposed reef. And when he looked back at the water, the dolphin had vanished. For some minutes, there was no trace of her. He felt the beginnings of panic. Had she marooned him? And if she had, how would he ever swim across the inlet by himself?

'Where are you?' he wanted to shout. 'I'm not Tim Benson. I can't see!'

But his panic was short-lived. As on the night she had drawn him to the beach, he heard her wild thrashing in the shallows. Slowly, he picked his way toward the commotion, stumbling through rock pools, creeping on all fours until he found her.

She was lying in the shallow water of a tiny bay, a cove where low waves swished and sucked at a miniature pebble beach, and when Seb looked about him, he knew exactly what the dolphin intended him to see. Backed by a steep wall of rock, only a few metres from the water, the cove held a secret cleft – a line of darkness against the black cliffs. He squinted. It was a narrow sea cave. And wedged across its entrance, Seb saw the blurred outline of an inflatable rubber life raft.

Margaret Beames

ARCHWAY ARROW

ILLUSTRATED BY CARLA SHALE

One thing's for sure – the Rainford Rats and their dirty tricks won't stop this team.

That afternoon Jamie returned to the pool for yet another session. He was sure he wasn't getting as breathless as he had at first. He didn't swallow as much water either. By the time he was ready to climb out he felt he was making real progress. He couldn't wait to see his mother's face when he told her he could swim a length.

Meanwhile Stefan, Colin and Scott were waiting for the girls in Colin's backyard.

'Where are they?' demanded Stefan impatiently. 'They said they'd bring the rope this afternoon.'

'It's OK, here they come,' said Colin.

Trish tossed a plastic shopping bag onto the grass. It clinked as it landed. 'Toggles,' she announced. 'We got them from my dad's store. And the rope.'

Annie had a long coil of thin yellow rope slung over her shoulder.

'That rope doesn't look very strong,' said Stefan.

'It is so,' retorted Annie. 'It's nylon. Trish's dad let us have it for four dollars, cost price.'

Scott had already grabbed one end and was starting to wind it around the first drum. 'Come and help,' he said to the others.

There was enough rope to go around all three drums several times, over and under like figures of eight, but it wasn't easy. Even with five people to handle them, the drums slipped and rolled awkwardly.

'Ouch!' yelled Trish as they ran over her foot.

'This is no good,' said Colin, nursing a pinched finger. 'There must be a better way.'

They stood back and stared at the three drums. 'I know,' said Stefan. 'It's simple. All we have to do is stand them on end so they can't roll. We can lie them down after they're lashed together.'

It was so obvious they felt stupid for not thinking of it before. Now the work went better. Soon the rope was pulled tight around the drums. Then they pushed them and they fell with a hollow crash onto their sides.

Scott checked the knots. 'Now for the planks,' he said.

Colin borrowed his father's largest hammer and with much noise and enthusiasm the boys bashed the toggles through the wood into the metal drums. Then they screwed the caps tightly onto the tops of the drums to keep the water out.

'The air inside'll keep them buoyant,' said Stefan confidently.

And there it was, one raft ready to launch. They leaped aboard in a wild victory dance. There was an ominous creak.

'Get off!' shouted Scott. 'It's cracking!'

They examined the raft for damage.

'It looks OK,' said Stefan. 'But from now on, no more than four people on it at one time and no stamping.'

'Where's Jamie? He ought to be here,' said Trish.

'Learning to swim,' Colin told her. 'His mother won't let him be in the team unless he can swim, and to prove it he has to be able to swim a length.'

Trish looked thoughtful, but she said nothing because at that moment Jamie came speeding down the drive on his bike.

'I did half a width –' he began, then stopped in amazement. 'You've done it! Wow!' He couldn't help feeling a pang of disappointment that they'd finished it without him.

'Yep,' said Stefan. 'Tomorrow we launch it.'

They could hardly wait. Fortunately Sunday was a fine sunny day, so there were no objections from their parents when they said they wanted to take the raft to the river. Even Jamie's mother let him go – with a warning to keep out of the water.

'How're you going to get it to the river?' asked Colin's father.

'Well,' said Colin, 'we were kind of hoping . . .' His father groaned. 'Why did I ask?'

'Please, Dad.'

His father sighed. 'All right. I'll hitch the trailer up, but once you're there you're on your own. I've got other things to do, you know.'

He helped them load the raft on to the trailer. The drums fitted snugly into the bed of the trailer with the wooden platform overlapping the sides slightly. Trish tied two old skipping ropes to the back as mooring lines, then they all piled into the car.

'Where to?' asked Colin's father.

'Do you know old Mr Thomas's house, on the river?' asked Stefan.

Colin's father nodded. 'Well, there's a good launching place near there. I saw it when we got the planks and it's not too far out of town.'

'I know it,' said Mr Bell. 'Here we go then.'

The river was wide and smooth-flowing, with muddy grass verges. Near Mr Thomas's property a wash-out had made a break in the bank that sloped smoothly down to shallow water. On the far side, a steep bank of bush rose out of deep, dark water. They left the road and bumped over the grass to the river path. They were not the only people who thought it was a good launching site. Two other rafts were already on the water and another was parked under the trees.

Mr Bell helped them lift their raft off the trailer, then he leaned against the car and watched.

One of the rafts in the water was made of old inner tubes. It bobbed and bounced and swung around in crazy circles as the tubes slipped against each other, and the paddlers slipped off the tubes into the water.

'They've tied it too loosely,' scoffed Scott.

'I bet it won't sink, though,' said Colin, with a doubtful glance at their own effort.

The other raft looked to be more of a threat. It was built of wood, with large fishing floats along the sides. The front was pointed to cut cleanly through the water and the crew was equipped with real canoe paddles. There was even a flag fluttering at the stern; a large, dark blue R stood out against the background of wavy, pale blue and white lines.

'Rainford Lodge,' groaned Scott. 'We might've known they'd have the best of everything.'

'There's Bains, bossing the others around,' said Colin. 'Trust him to be captain.'

'They're even dressed the same,' said Trish.

'And look at the size of them,' added Jamie, taking in the muscular arms and legs of the crew in their dark blue shorts and light blue shirts.

'So what?' Annie said suddenly. 'Looks aren't everything. We can beat them.'

'Not by standing on the bank, we can't,' said Stefan. 'Come on, don't worry about the Rainford Rats. Let's get this tub into the water.'

The Rainford boys were watching from midstream, grinning and nudging each other and making remarks that the Archway team couldn't quite hear, but which were obviously insulting. They tried to ignore the other team as they dragged the raft towards the river.

They pushed and heaved their raft into the shallows, where it rode high and steady. The smiles on the Rainford faces faded a little.

'Jamie, you'd better stay here,' Annie reminded him. 'Remember what your mother said. I'll go in your place.'

'Oh no, you won't,' said Jamie. 'And I'm not going *in* the river, I'm going *on* it. Anyway, the water's only up to our knees here. I could hardly drown in that, could I?'

'Oh, let him go,' said Trish, looking doubtfully at the way the raft bobbed about. 'We'll wait until we see how it floats. We haven't even got paddles yet, remember.'

Trish and Annie held the ropes as the current swung the raft out into the deeper water. The boys waded out to it.

'Better all climb on together,' suggested Stefan. 'One at each corner. Ready? Go.'

With fingers digging at the lashing they scrambled aboard, kneeling on the rough planks, feeling suddenly very unsafe. Colin yelped as a splinter stabbed into his knee. He shifted his weight onto the other leg while he tried to pull it out. The raft began to wobble. It gave a lurch. Then before they knew what was happening it flipped over and there they were, floundering in the water while the three oil drums rode high above the wooden platform, which was now completely submerged.

Jamie gasped as the cold water rushed into his eyes and ears. It filled his mouth and he began to choke. He thrashed about in panic. He was going to drown! Suddenly a firm hand grabbed his collar and hauled him upright. He spat out a mouthful of river water.

'Ugh! I swallowed something. I felt it go down,' he spluttered.

'Did it wriggle?' Scott grinned without sympathy.

Jamie looked around and saw Stefan and Colin hanging on to the raft, stopping it drifting away. Like Scott, and now himself, they were standing only waist deep in the water.

With shrieks of hysterical laughter from the Rainford crew ringing in their ears, the boys waded ashore, towing the raft behind them. Trish and Annie were clutching each other and giggling helplessly, while beside the car Mr Bell was roaring and wiping tears from his eyes.

'It's not that funny!' yelled Colin. 'And you knew that would happen, Dad. Why didn't you warn us?'

'Because you wouldn't have believed me.' Mr Bell tried to be serious. 'This way you've seen for yourselves. Here, use these.'

He threw them a bundle of old towels. Guessing what would happen, he'd tossed them into the car at the last moment. While Trish and Annie hauled the raft ashore and with Mr Bell's help turned it right way up, the boys stripped off their wet clothes and dried themselves.

They wrapped the towels around their waists and spread their clothes in the sun to dry.

'What're you going to call it? The *Archway Ark*?' jeered Bains from the Rainford raft that was floating high and dry in mid-river.

'They're going to wear frogmen suits and push it from underneath,' sniggered another boy.

'Get lost,' was the best Stefan could think of. It didn't sound much of a threat, even to him.

'So what now?' asked Trish.

Stefan sighed. 'Back to the drawing board and start again, I suppose. This thing's useless now, isn't it?'

They all looked so dejected that Mr Bell took pity on them.

'Not at all,' he said. 'Let me get that splinter out for you, Colin, and we'll see what can be done.'

Laura Ranger

AUTUMN GOLD

The money tree flings the leaves down
the dollars flutter to the ground,

the notes are lying in deep heaps
they look as messy as my bedroom

I'm climbing the bank
and rustling in the leaves

I go mining for gold.

William Taylor

KNITWITS

*What if the guys on his hockey team find out
that Charlie has made a bet to knit something?*

Do I wish to share my life with a baby?

The answer is a flat no, and I'm not being selfish at all.

He'll be into nicking everything I own and want all my things in no time flat. In no time flat he'll be after all my stuff. In no time flat he'll be into my T-shirts and sweatshirts and even think he's big enough to fit my jeans and sneakers.

Grandma says having a baby is a bit like a raffle and she's hoping Mum will come up with a better prize the second time around, and doesn't Mum think she's bought one too many tickets already. Grandma says she can't understand why she seems to have been the last to be told the happy news.

Alice Pepper has confirmed my very worst unspoken fears. The baby could be a girl! 'Least then I'd have someone sensible to talk to and share secrets with. It's all boys round here and that's pure puke. My mum knew your mum was pregnant.'

'She did not so.'

'She did.'

'She didn't.'

'She did. She told me. She said she saw your mum was getting as fat round the middle as she already is round her bum. She said you could even tell it in that ad on the telly where she wears next to nothing and tips all that milk down that guy's throat and says "Cool as . . . Cool as milk," in what she thinks is a sexy voice. She could even tell in that ad.'

'Mum did that one last year and wasn't even pregnant then unless ladies are pregnant for just about two years and that's impossible,' I said.

'No it's not and elephants are and Mum says she could tell your mum was going to try and get pregnant and it was written all over her. What you going to make for your baby?' asked Alice.

'Nuthin'.'

'You've got to,' said Alice Pepper. 'It's the law. It'll be your little sister. You're gonna be the poor little devil's brother.'

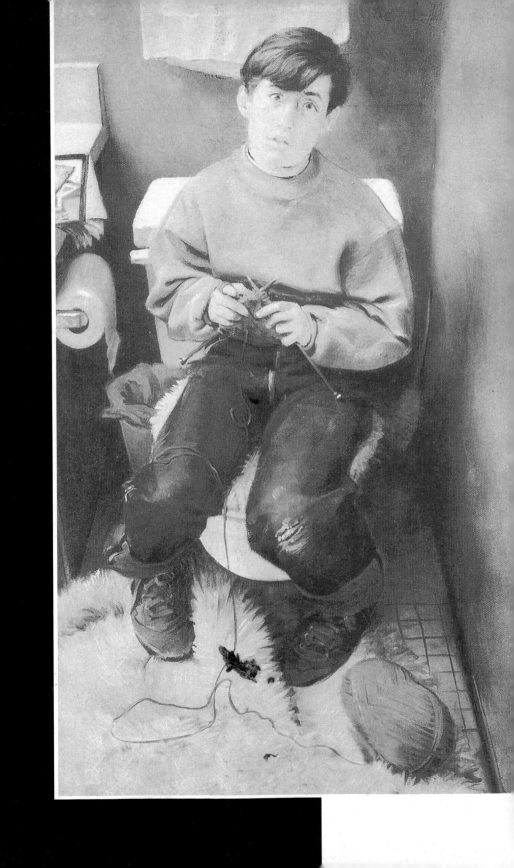

'It'll be my brother.'

'It's a girl,' said Alice Pepper. 'I can always tell.'

'I'm gonna knit him a sweater,' I said.

'You're gonna WHAT!!!?'

'You heard me,' I said. But why why why had I said it? Why? I must be double mad. Can I knit? Of course I can't knit! Alice Pepper does that sort of thing to me. Still, everyone knits junk for poor babies. Why not me?

'You? Knit? Bet you don't.'

'Bet I do. I just bet I can knit something for a baby,' I said.

'Bet you can't.'

'How much d'you bet?'

'A thousand million trillion dollars,' said Alice Pepper.

'You haven't got that much.'

'Yeah. And you can't knit, either. I know. So there!' said Alice Pepper. 'So I'll bet all my collections, every one of them, every single one of them, that you can't knit your baby a sweater.'

Wow! WOW!! Alice Pepper is one bigtime collector. Alice Pepper has got a bottle top collection, a beer can collection, a paper napkin collection, a light bulb collection, a matchbox collection, a dead insect collection, and an old coin collection. Alice Pepper has also got the prize collection of all, the most brilliant and awesome collection of all – a skull collection.

Alice Pepper owns the skulls of a sparrow, a starling, a parrot, a mouse, a rat, a chicken, a duck, a rabbit, a possum, a cat, a dog, a hare, a sheep, a goat (with horns), a horse, a deer (with one horn), and a cow (with half a horn). Alice Pepper says it's only a matter of time before she gets hold of the skulls of a monkey and a human, and she's working on both. Well, I know it's only a matter of time for the human one. Alice Pepper has told me that after about a hundred years human skulls that have been buried with their owners start popping up to the surface in cemeteries. Once they've left the rest of their owner they're anyone's. Our cemetery is about a hundred years old and we go there quite often, her and me, just to check if the first skull has popped up. So far it hasn't.

'And when you lose, which you will, you can give me five dollars a week for the rest of my life and no matter how long I live,' said Alice Pepper.

'I don't get five dollars a week,' I said.

'Then I'll just put it all down in a notebook until you do, even if you go on the dole and you probably will,' said Alice Pepper. 'And I'm gonna charge you interest.'

'You're on,' I said, and stuck out my hand.

'Oh, no no no. You don't get away with it easy as that,' said Alice. 'This is a big one, a very big one. You gotta shake three times.'

So we shook hands three times and swore we'd go to hell and get our throats slit if we told a lie about it.

'Aaaahhh . . .' Alice Pepper let out a big satisfied sigh. 'Five bucks a week for life. Always knew you were a sucker and now you proved it. Like taking money from a baby, and I reckon that's sort of what I am doing.'

'Don't you bet on it, Pepper,' I said, and jumped the hedge that separates our houses in some places. 'I can so knit. I can knit real good.'

'No you can't, sucker. So there. And you never ever will. Five bucks a week for life, sucker.'

'It's gonna be a surprise and don't you tell no one I'm knittin' a sweater. Not the guys. Not Jacko and Spikey.'

'Wouldn't tell them their faces look like the bum of an ape and they do,' said Alice Pepper.

Alice Pepper did not like the guys. The guys did not like Alice Pepper. The only living creature who could beat Jacko and Spikey and me in anything, even in a fight, was Alice Pepper, my girl next door.

Anthony Holcroft

THE TRAMP

ILLUSTRATED BY ELSPETH WILLIAMSON

There was a farmer whose well had run dry. For days he searched for a fresh supply of water, but with no luck. Things were looking bad. The grass had dried up, the sheep were skin-and-bone, and the cow wouldn't give any milk. In his despair he leaned on the gate and called on the heavens to take pity. 'Send her down, Huey, and I'll be a better man ever after!'

But not a drop fell from the pitiless sky. There was not a cloud on the horizon. Then he noticed that someone was walking towards him up the road. 'Maybe it's old Huey himself,' said the farmer, 'come down to answer my prayers with a bucket of water.' But it was only a tramp, a dirty, dusty old tramp with clickety-clack boots and pants tied up with a piece of string.

'Gooday there, Squire,' said the tramp, resting his foot on the gate. 'And what a fine, beautiful morning it is, too. Not a cloud in the sky.' 'It doesn't look too good from where I'm standing,' grunted the farmer. 'Ah,' said the tramp, 'but these are hard times we live in.

Look at me, now – I haven't had a square meal for two whole days. Fair ravening, I am.' He took out a little pipe and began puffing on it. The air seemed suddenly full of crackling broom pods. 'Tell you what, Squire,' said the tramp, 'you couldn't spare a crust, could you?'

The farmer gave the tramp a look that was none too friendly.

'If you want a crust, you'll have to earn it,' he said gruffly.

With a bound the tramp leapt over the gate. 'Whatever you say, boss, whatever you say. I can turn my hand to anything.'

'Fine,' said the farmer. 'Then how about finding me some good fresh water? My well's dried up.'

'As soon as done,' said the tramp. He broke a branch from a nearby willow tree and began walking across the paddock holding the stick before him. Suddenly the stick began jumping around in his hand. 'Dig your well here,' said the tramp. The farmer did so, and water gushed out of the ground – enough and more to water his land. He leapt in the air for joy. 'I'm saved!' he shouted, 'home and hosed!'

In his excitement the farmer had forgotten all about the tramp. But suddenly there was a tap on his shoulder. The tramp stood there, puffing on his pipe. 'Can I have that crust, Boss?' he asked.

The farmer gave him a crafty look. 'Sure you can. But first you'll have to milk my cow.'

'No problem,' said the tramp, 'but I'll need a big bucket, the biggest you've got.'

Smiling to himself, the farmer went away and fetched a large slop bucket. The tramp then proceeded to milk the cow, whistling a strange little tune between his teeth. The cow must have liked the tune, because the milk poured out; it over-flowed. The farmer had to run and fetch another bucket – and another. There was no end to it. 'Stop!' he shouted at last. 'You'll drown us all in milk!'

The tramp smiled and rubbed his hands. 'Now can I have that crust, Boss?' said he. 'I've a space in my belly the size of a bucket.' 'All in good time,' said the farmer. 'But first I want you to pick my apple tree.'

The tramp squinted up at the tree. It was very tall and tangled, and what little fruit there was, was clustered at the top. But that was no problem. 'I'll want a big basket, though,' said the tramp, 'the biggest you've got.' 'You must be joking,' said the farmer. 'What's up there would hardly fill that hat of yours.' But he brought the basket all the same. Then the tramp gave the tree a good shake, and the apples came tumbling down. Some fell on the ground, some in the basket, which was soon overflowing. The farmer ran for another basket, and another. Soon they were full too, yet still the apples tumbled.

'All right!' shouted the farmer. 'That'll do! You'll have us all buried in apples.' He stared at the great mound of fruit lying under the apple tree. 'I would never have believed it,' he muttered.

'And nor would I,' says a voice beside him. 'So how about that tasty crust, Boss? Right now I could go some spuds and peas, and a nice little sliver of lamb in mint sauce.'

'All in good time, all in good time,' says the farmer. 'There's still the sheep to shear.'

The tramp's face darkened suddenly. 'Sheep is it?' he growled. 'I'll give you sheep!' He stamped his foot once, and to his amazement the farmer saw that all the sheep had fleeces of pure gold. He stamped his foot twice, and the milk turned to cream in the pails and the fruit in the baskets to silver. He stamped a third time, and red wine gushed from the spring. 'There!' says the tramp. 'Happy now?' And he walked away.

The farmer, who had been grovelling on the ground for the gold and silver, ran after him and thrust a loaf of fresh-baked bread into his hand. 'You're forgetting your crust,' says he. 'A promise is a promise, and I always keep my word.'

The tramp winked solemnly as he stowed the bread in his shirt. 'Have a good day,' said he, and walked on his way.

The farmer rubbed his hands. 'That was a good deal,' he said to himself. 'He got his crust and I certainly got more than I bargained for.'

But when he got back there was no sign of wine, nor cream, nor silver apples. He ran to the well. It was dusty dry. The apple tree was bare, the fleeces had withered on the sheep. And when he tried to milk the cow, he was unable to squeeze a single drop into the pail.

'Tramps!' muttered the farmer. 'You can never trust them! And to think he got away with a loaf of my best bread! Wait till I catch him!'

But he never did.

David Hill

THE WINNING TOUCH

ILLUSTRATED BY JEFFREY PARKER

When Welton Intermediate School starts its own New Image rugby team, things don't look promising . . .

Friday afternoon, it started to rain. It rained all afternoon and most of that night. When five car-loads of Welton parents and kids reached Kaimana Valley School on Saturday morning (Holly's parents were at the Motorbike Expo), the rain had almost stopped, but a cool wind was blowing.

'Look at the field!' gasped Tammy. 'It's a swamp!'

The Kaimana Valley playing field was a brown oblong of mud, with a few grassy tufts poking up and little pools of water lying in the footprints. The field next to it, where another game was just starting, looked almost as bad.

'If we fall over in that, we'll really be All Blacks,' said Dean.

'I'll get mud in my hair,' complained Silina.

'Never mind,' said Tu helpfully. 'So will Murdoch.'

A voice like a grizzly bear growled from behind them. 'You kids better try these jerseys,' Ira's father said.

Mr Esera opened the top of a black plastic rubbish bag and began lifting out jerseys three at a time.

'Orange and purple,' murmured Ms Benge. 'Out of this world!'

Ani and Tammy chose two jerseys exactly the same size. Dean removed his glasses, pulled on a jersey, found his glasses and discovered he'd put his jersey on inside out. Ira just managed to squeeze the biggest jersey over his shoulders. Murdoch refused two jerseys because they were crumpled, then found a neatly folded one. Holly put on the smallest jersey and stood around grinning – it almost reached her knees before she tucked it in.

'Silina – reserve for the first half, please,' said Mr O'Neill. Silina looked almost relieved as she watched the others step out onto the muddy field.

The first half was a shambles. Dean passed to Murdoch; Murdoch tried to swerve left, then swerve right. Instead he skidded in the

mud and swerved squelch! onto his backside.

Not long afterwards, Ira intercepted a pass, ran a little way, then passed to Tammy. Trouble was, Ira kept sliding in the mud even after he'd passed the ball. He slid for another ten metres, rumbling like a runaway tank and knocking two Kaimana Valley kids flying as he did so.

Suddenly, there was a shriek from one of the Kaimana Valley girls: 'Thtop! I've lotht my tooth. My falth tooth.'

The game came to a halt while twenty players, plus the Kaimana Valley coach who was refereeing the first half, searched around in the mud. Finally, Shayne held up a small muddy white square with plastic hooks on it.

'Thath it!' exclaimed the Kaimana girl. 'My plathtic fantathtic. Thankth.' And while the Welton team watched, eyes and mouths round, she wiped the tooth on her shorts and slipped it back into her mouth.

By half-time the Welton Wonderers had scored one try, thanks to Dallas being on the spot when one of the Kaimana Valley girls dropped the slippery ball. Kaimana had also scored a try, thanks to one of their girls being on the spot when Dallas dropped the slippery ball.

'Got any hot pies, Ms Benge?' asked Tu.

'Never mind hot pies,' Mr O'Neill said. 'Let's have lots of short passes this half. Short passes and calling for the ball like we've practised. It's too slippery to try long passes.'

Tu was reserve for the second half, although Silina insisted she didn't mind sitting out the whole game. 'It's okay,' said Tu. 'I haven't got a cousin in this team, anyway.'

Mr O'Neill was right. The short passes and calling for the ball worked. People still dropped the ball and slipped in the mud, but good tries were scored by Tammy, Shayne ('Good on ya, tooth fairy!' yelled Tu from the sideline), Murdoch and Ira, who kept on sliding after he'd forced the ball, almost flattening two spectators. Murdoch converted two of the tries despite the wet, heavy ball. Kaimana Valley got one more try and Welton won 29-14.

The score could have been 34-14. Midway through the second half, Dean got the ball and set off on a curving, swerving, flying run. While the other Welton players yelled and shouted, Dean tore past three staring opposition players and over the goal line. Only trouble was, without his glasses, Dean had made his curving, swerving, flying run across onto the next field where the other game was in progress, and he scored over the next field's goal line.

'You guys are good, all right,' Tammy's father smiled as his try-scoring daughter and the others were gratefully putting on warm sweatshirts and jackets after the game was over. 'You must be good if you can afford to score tries for other teams as well!'

Jennifer Beck

THE BANTAM AND
THE SOLDIER

(EXTRACT)
ILLUSTRATED BY ROBYN BELTON

Arthur never talked much about the war, but one day
he said to his niece, 'I want to tell you a story . . .
about a bantam I called Bertha.'

Arthur has just rescued
a little bantam from
a tree . . .

That evening, Arthur fed the
bantam some food he had
saved. The other soldiers
shook their heads and laughed
at him.

'What's the use of keeping that miserable looking bird?' one of them demanded. 'It's so scrawny, it wouldn't even make a decent bowl of soup!'

'If it starts crowing in the night, I'll wring its skinny neck!' warned another.

'Her name is Bertha,' replied Arthur, 'and she needs someone to look after her.'

At first, life in the trenches was not so bad. Arthur was able to share his food with Bertha, and she grew stronger. The soldiers stopped teasing Arthur, and began to look upon Bertha as a lucky mascot. They even helped him build a pen for her.

But the fighting grew heavier. Food became scarce, and Arthur and his companions collected grubs and worms for Bertha from the muddy banks of their clay prison.

And she rewarded them. In the midst of a raging battle, when the sky was crisscrossed with fire, Bertha laid a warm brown egg. When Arthur found it, he hugged the little bantam to his mud-caked jacket.

Every morning from then on, as regular as daybreak, Bertha laid an egg for Arthur and his friends. They shared the eggs, a treat for those who were most in need. During the terrible weeks that followed, the bantam gave them something to joke about. 'A hen in the trench is worth five on the farm,' they'd say, or 'An egg a day keeps the shell shock away.'

Above all, Bertha gave the soldiers courage and hope. 'If a bantam can live through this, and lay eggs as well,' they told one another, 'then perhaps we can survive this terrible war.'

ANZAC BISCUITS

125 g butter   1 cup rolled oats
1 cup flour   2 Tbsp golden syrup
1 cup sugar   1 tsp baking soda
½ cup dessicated coconut   2 Tbsp boiling water

· Gently melt butter and golden syrup together
· Combine flour, sugar, coconut and rolled oats
  in a separate bowl.
· Dissolve the baking soda in the boiling water
  and add to butter and golden syrup.
· Stir into the dry ingredients.
· Place in spoonfuls on a baking tray, allowing
  room for the mixture to spread.

Bake at 180°C for 14-20 minutes.

Joy Watson

GRANDPA'S SLIPPERS

ILLUSTRATED BY WENDY HODDER

On Monday,
Grandma looked at Grandpa's old slippers.
'You need new slippers,' she said.
'Those are going to fall to bits.'

'Nonsense,' said Grandpa.
'My slippers are fine.'

'But they have holes in their soles,' said Grandma.
'Good,' said Grandpa. 'That's how I like them.'

Nevertheless,
Grandma bought him a new pair of slippers that day.
Grandpa refused to wear them.

On Tuesday,
Grandpa was cleaning out
the cupboard under the stairs
when he came upon his old slippers
hidden away in the darkest corner.

'Leave my slippers alone,' he told Grandma.
'Don't try to hide them!'

'They should be hidden,'
said Grandma.

'They're going to fall to bits.
They have holes in their soles
and the stitching has come
undone.'

'Good,' said Grandpa.
'That's how I like them.'

On Wednesday,
Grandpa was just in time
to see Grandma handing his old slippers
to a person collecting used clothing.

'Hey! Leave my slippers alone,' he told Grandma.
'Don't try to give them away!'

'They should be given away,'
said Grandma.

'They're going to fall to bits.
They have holes in their soles,
the stitching has come undone
and all the fluff has worn off.'

'Good,' said Grandpa. 'That's how I like them.'

On Thursday,
Grandpa went to check
if the rubbish bag had been put out.
There, right on the top, were his old slippers.

'Do leave my slippers alone,' he told Grandma.
'Don't try to throw them away.'

'They should be thrown away,' said Grandma.
'They're going to fall to bits.
They have holes in their soles,
the stitching has come undone,
all the fluff has worn off
and I can see your toes.'

'Good,' said Grandpa.
'That's how I like them.'

On Friday,
Grandpa took some potato peelings
out to the compost heap.
There, not quite covered by a cabbage leaf,
were his old slippers.

'Please leave my slippers alone,'
he told Grandma.
'Don't try to bury them in the
   compost heap!'

'They should be buried,'
said Grandma.
'They're going to fall to bits.
They have holes in their soles,
the stitching has come undone,
all the fluff has worn off
and I can see your toes.
They're so tatty.'

'Good,' said Grandpa.
'That's how I like them.'

On Saturday,
Grandpa was just about to set fire
to a pile of leaves in the garden
when a sudden gust of wind revealed
– his old slippers!

'Oh, no!' said Grandpa, and he told Grandma,
'Once and for all,
will you please leave my old slippers alone.
Don't try to burn them.'

'Very well, but they should be burned,'
said Grandma.
'They're going to fall to bits.
They have holes in their soles,
the stitching has come undone,
all the fluff has worn off
and I can see your toes.
They're *so* tatty
and they look very uncomfortable.'

'Good,' said Grandpa. 'That's how I like them.'

On Sunday morning,
Grandpa got out of bed
and was about to put on his old slippers
when they fell to bits in his hands!

He had to wear his new slippers instead.

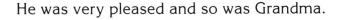

They had whole soles,
strong stitching,
warm fluff covering his toes
and they looked neat and natty.
Grandpa was surprised to find
that they were actually very comfortable indeed.

He was very pleased and so was Grandma.

On Monday,
Grandma looked at Grandpa's old grey cardigan.

'You need a new cardigan,' she said.

Gaelyn Gordon

DUCKAT

ILLUSTRATED BY CHRIS GASKIN

On Monday morning, Mabel opened her door. There was a duck on the back step. 'Hello,' said Mabel. 'Meow,' said the duck.

'Odd,' said Mabel. 'Very odd.'

She put it in the lily pond. But it hated that. 'Yeowwww!' it yelled. 'I've never been scratched by a duck before,' said Mabel.

The duck would not eat bread, but it drank a bowl full of milk. It caught five mice and gave them to Mabel. 'Odd,' said Mabel. 'Very odd.' When the duck wasn't looking, Mabel hid the mice in the bread bin. 'I don't want to hurt its feelings,' she said.

The duck hid under the sofa and pounced at Mabel's toes. 'Well!' said Mabel. 'You are a very different sort of duck.'

When Mabel started knitting, the
duck joined in. It growled at the balls of yarn, and stalked
them like a mighty hunter. It rolled them over the floor. 'Odd,' said
Mabel. 'Very odd.'

The duck curled up by the fire and purred a bit. Then it went to
sleep. 'That duck,' said Mabel, 'thinks it's a cat.' She got out her
Doctor Book and looked up: *What to do for a duck that thinks
it is a cat.*

When the duck woke up, there were pictures all around it. There were pictures of ducks labelled DUCK, and pictures of cats labelled CAT. The duck changed the labels over.

'Well!' said Mabel. 'What do I have to do to show you that you're a duck?' The duck shrugged. 'Meow,' it said.

Mabel took the duck outside. 'Cats climb trees,' she said. The duck climbed the tree. 'Odd,' said Mabel. 'Very odd.'

'Cats wash behind their ears,' said Mabel. The duck washed behind
its ears. 'Odd,' said Mabel. 'Very odd.'

Butch, the dog who lived next door, bounced through the gate. 'Dogs
chase cats,' said Mabel. 'But they chase ducks, too.' Butch nearly
got the duck, but it flew up to the top of the lamppost. 'You couldn't
do that if you were a cat,' said Mabel.

Mabel pushed Butch through the gate and locked it. 'You can come
down now,' Mabel told the duck. 'Meow,' said the duck. 'Cats can't
fly down from lampposts,' said Mabel, 'and I don't have a ladder. If
you are a cat, you'll just have to stay up there.' The duck flew down.
It looked up at Mabel. 'Quack,' it said. 'You were only joking, weren't
you?' said Mabel.

'Quack,' said the duck, and it went for
a swim in the lily pond to cool off.

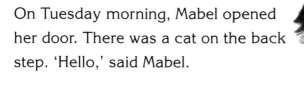

On Tuesday morning, Mabel opened
her door. There was a cat on the back
step. 'Hello,' said Mabel.

'Quack!' said the cat.

'Odd,' said the duck. 'Very odd.'

Patricia Grace

THE KUIA
AND THE SPIDER

ILLUSTRATED BY ROBYN KAHUKIWA

Once there was a kuia who made mats and baskets. In the corner of her kitchen lived a spider who made webs. One day the spider called out to the kuia, 'Hey old woman, my weaving is better than yours.' The kuia called back to the spider, 'Spider, your weaving is koretake, it's only good for catching flies.'

'Yours is only good for sitting on,' called the spider. And they argued and argued.

At last the spider said to the kuia, 'I'll tell you what, we'll have a weaving competition.'

'Yes,' said the kuia. 'And when our grandchildren come on Saturday they'll tell us whose weaving is best.' So the spider and the kuia stopped arguing and got to work. The kuia made mats to sit on and mats to sleep on. She made kits for kumara, kits for seafood, kits

for shopping, and kits for giving away to her family and friends.

The spider made webs for catching flies in, and webs for wrapping food in. He made webs for climbing up, and webs for swinging on. He made an enormous web over the window that looked beautiful when the sun shone on it.

The kuia and the spider worked every day and every night until it was Saturday. On Saturday morning the kuia's grandchildren came, and the spider's grandchildren came. 'Whose weaving is best?' asked the kuia. But the kuia's grandchildren did not answer. They sat on the mats and sang songs. They lay on the mats and talked. They took kits to the garden and got kumara. They took kits to the beach and got pipis. They took kits to the shop and got coffee. They found kits with their names on them and held on to them tightly.

'Whose weaving is best?' asked the spider. But the spider's grandchildren did not answer. They caught flies in the webs and had a party. They wrapped flies' heads in the webs and hid them away. They went climbing all over the kitchen on the climbing webs. They went swinging from wall to wall on the swinging webs. They sat and stared at the enormous web over the window that shone in the sun.

Then the kuia's grandchildren went to sleep on the sleeping mats. And the spider's grandchildren went to sleep in the enormous web over the window. 'You see, my weaving is better than yours,' said the kuia. 'If my grandchildren went to sleep in your weaving they would fall and hurt themselves.'

'No, no, my weaving is better than yours,' said the spider. 'If my grandchildren slept on your weaving someone would tread on them and squash them.' And they argued and argued until the kuia said to the spider, 'Spider, I'm sick of you. I think I'll go and live out in the wash-house.' But she didn't, she went to sleep by her grandchildren. And the spider said to the kuia, 'Old woman, you make me mad. I think I'll go and live in someone else's kitchen.' But he didn't, he went to sleep by his grandchildren.

The next morning they all woke up, and the spider called out to the kuia, 'Hey, you, old woman, my grandchildren are better than yours.'

'Hoha,' yelled the kuia.
'Your grandchildren are HOHA.
My grandchildren are much
better than yours.'

And they argued and
argued and argued for
the rest of their lives.

hoha   a nuisance
koretake: useless, to no purpose
kuia: old woman, grandmother

Sherryl Jordan

SIGN OF THE LION

PHOTOGRAPHY BY STEPHEN ROBINSON

A haunting tale of ambition and the power of faith.

Minstrel stood staring at them all, her heart thumping like a drum. Something terrible hung in the shadows of the chilly house, something to do with the woman in the chair who rocked back and forth and smiled. Minstrel feared her smile and the way the woman's strange eyes gleamed in the semi-dark.

For a while no one moved or spoke. Then Minstrel's mother came over and put a trembling arm across her shoulder.

'Tell her, Thomas,' her mother said to Minstrel's father. 'Tell your only child what you've done to her.' Her voice was harsh and cold, and Minstrel had never heard it like this before. Panic filled her.

'What, Father?' Minstrel asked. 'What did you do?'

But Thomas was shaking his head and crying, his hands held out pleadingly towards his wife. 'I did it for you, Catherine,' he said hoarsely. 'For you! If I hadn't, you would have died. You both would have died. I did it for love of *you*!'

'Did what?' cried Minstrel.

'You knew how wrong, how evil it was!' Catherine shouted. 'Yet you still did it! And you never told me, for shame! And all these years I thought you loved us – loved us *both* – and all the time your evil pledge was hanging over us!'

'I forgot it!' Thomas cried. 'I worried at first, but then when the babe grew and we were so happy together, I thought it was all forgotten, like a nightmare, like your pain. I forgot it. I never dreamed –'

'*Forgot what?*' screamed Minstrel.

There was a sudden silence. Then only the creak of the rocking chair, as it rocked back and forth, back and forth.

At last Minstrel's mother spoke.

'He made a promise about you, Minstrel, when you were born,' she said. 'He swore a solemn vow that when you were twelve years old he would give you away.'

Minstrel's world blurred and the room seemed to spin about her. All she could see was the strange woman's gloating smile and her weird, unearthly eyes.

'Give me away?' Minstrel choked. 'You would give me away? To *her*?'

'She helped me at your borning time,' said her mother, her voice strangely calm, though tears poured down her cheeks. 'I was nearly dead. Your father had gone for help and was away all the night. Then he returned, with her. She was so kind, Minstrel. She gave me medicines and talked me through the pain, and when you finally came she held you in her arms and said what a beautiful, special daughter you were. Then she placed you against my breast and went away. All these years I have loved her and thanked God for her, and for you. And now she has come back.'

'Well, she can go away again – by herself,' said Minstrel.

'Hush, don't speak that way,' said Catherine. 'We are talking of a solemn pledge made on my life, and it cannot be broken. You have no say in the matter.'

'I will not go!'

'You have to, my darling,' said her father quietly. 'Your mother is right. But I promise we will come and visit you as many times as – '

'Take great care with your promises,' said the woman in the rocking chair. 'You have already found one pledge a little difficult to keep. The child is mine now. You will not visit her or send her messages or have anything else to do with her ever again. You have surrendered her to me. You no longer have the right to call her your daughter.'

'You have no right, either!' Minstrel shouted at her. 'You're talking about *me*. Not an old goat or a basket or eggs! *Me*! And I won't go away with you! I belong here.'

Slowly the woman turned to face Minstrel, and her eyes were so frightening that the girl almost turned and fled. She heard her mother give a little cry and move away. Minstrel stood her ground, staring at the woman, her heart thundering and her mouth dry.

To her relief, Elmo appeared, standing near the far wall, opposite the woman in the rocking chair. His radiance poured across the gloomy room, flooding the abandoned borning-day meal on the table and making it seem as if Minstrel herself stood in a ray of sun. The light flooded the floor all the way to the rocking chair, where it stopped just short of the woman's feet.

So intense was the beam, Minstrel was certain that everyone else must surely see it. But Catherine had closed her eyes and was murmuring a prayer for help, and Thomas had slumped onto a low stool and covered his face with his hands. Only the strange woman seemed to be aware, for she had leaned forward and was staring towards the place where Elmo was. She was breathing unevenly and her hands were clenched on the arms of the chair, as if she

were distressed. For a wonderful moment Minstrel thought she was going to get up and flee. But after a while the woman looked at Minstrel again, and her eyes were more terrible, more cold and relentless, than ever.

'I will not leave without you, Minstrel,' the woman said, standing up. Minstrel was shocked to see how tall she was. She was all in shadow, because Elmo's light, though it illuminated everything else in the room, did not touch her.

'You cannot defy me,' the woman said, very quietly. 'I am Griselda. That's what you must call me, though I'm mother and father to you now. Go and pack some things in a chest. You must bring everything you want, because you won't be back. And don't think of running away and hiding from me, for that is impossible. I always find what I seek.'

'No!' cried Minstrel. 'I'll never leave with you!'

'Do as she says, dear one,' said Elmo. 'Now is not the time for battle.'

In disbelief, Minstrel stared at him. Elmo was serious.

'You're supposed to be my guardian!' Minstrel wailed. 'You're supposed to protect me! Go on! Throw her out!'

Minstrel's father, thinking Minstrel was speaking to him, lifted his head. 'I cannot fight her,' he said. 'No one can. She has powers you

– we – know nothing of. Besides, I cannot go back on a solemn oath I gave twelve years ago.'

'Your father speaks wisely for once,' said Griselda. 'Go and pack your things, Minstrel. Now! Or you'll leave with nothing.'

Minstrel gazed at Elmo, longing for deliverance. But he only nodded for Minstrel to do as she was told, his eyes full of sorrow and love.

Feeling utterly betrayed, Minstrel turned and went upstairs to the loft that was her sleeping place. Anger and grief swept through her, so strong that she hardly knew what she was doing. Moving more by touch than by sight in the darkness, she opened a small wooden chest at the foot of her bed, pulled out the clothes in it, and began filling it with the things she loved best. She put in the feather quilt her mother had made her, a candlestick she had made herself, and a tattered book her grandfather had given her. She could read only a little, but she loved the pictures in the book because they were of knights and dragons, kings and heroes – the stuff of Minstrel's dreams. She took her reed pipe from her pocket, wrapped it in her favourite shawl, and put it in the chest. The chest was almost full and she had packed no clothes yet. She stood staring around her place, her chestnut curls almost brushing the thatched roof.

There were heavy footsteps on the stairs, and her father came onto the loft, carrying a lamp. He placed it on a shelf in the wall, then sat on the edge of the bed. He was carrying something wrapped in a yellow cloth, and he held the bundle out to Minstrel. She turned away and went on cramming things into the chest, not caring what she was throwing in.

'I'm sorry, my darling,' said her father. 'She helped us and it was only afterwards that she told me what her price was, what I had to give her in payment. I didn't know until it was too late. She tricked me.'

'You still would have promised,' said Minstrel bitterly, brushing away tears and throwing a useless, threadbare stocking into the chest. 'You still would have asked her to help. You wouldn't have cared about me so long as you had Mother. You always loved her more than me. You never loved me at all.'

'That's not true,' said Thomas. 'I love you with all my heart. I swear I'll do everything I can to get you back.'

'Don't bother. I'll be happy with Griselda. At least *she* wants me.'

Elmo appeared, sitting shoulder to shoulder with the man on the bed. Unaware of the angel, the man bent his head in his hands and sighed deeply.

'Make peace with your father,' said Elmo. 'Don't part like this. You will regret it.'

Minstrel ignored him.

Thomas unfolded the bundle and held something out to his daughter.

It was a pair of boots, brand-new. Minstrel took them, stroking the soft blue leather and sniffing at the earthy leather smells. The boots were beautiful. For a moment or two she was tempted, then she dropped the boots on the floor, away from the chest.

Thomas stood and trudged down the stairs again. He was stooped, as if in the last hour he had aged twenty years. The sight of him made Minstrel's heart ache, but she would not call him back. She took the clothes out of the overflowing chest, chose only the few things she really wanted and packed them carefully in.

'I know it seems as if everything has gone wrong,' said Elmo gently. 'But all is well and nothing can happen to you that is not, for an extremely good reason, permitted to happen.'

'I don't believe you!' she whispered furiously. 'I don't understand anything anymore! Why are you telling me to do what she says? *Why*? Why aren't you doing anything to stop her?'

'Because, at least for a short time, it is necessary for you to be with her. No harm will come to you, I swear. I will be with you every moment, protecting you. Right now you must be obedient and trust me.'

'Trust you? How can I? You're supposed to save me from things like this! You're supposed to be my guardian! And right when I really need you, you can't do anything! I'd have been better off with a dog – at least that would have bitten her!'

'Biting the enemy's ankles would achieve nothing,' said Elmo. 'What is necessary is total victory through battle, nothing less. You did not hear what I said, Berenice.' He had called her by her true birth-name, and Minstrel stopped what she was doing and listened, for when he used her real name his words were serious. 'This time is necessary,' he said. 'But take great care, for the enemy is strong and treacherous and very cunning. Do not listen to her, for she will lie. She's a clever liar and will mix deceptions with deepest truths. She'll try to confuse and deceive you. Play your music often, especially the tunes I taught you. Remember them every moment, and hold to the peace that is in them. If you begin to forget them it means that she is winning you over. She mustn't do that. Hold fast to everything you know, everything you love. And trust in my power. When the time is right, I will rescue you.'

'Will I see you when I'm with her?'

'Not all the time, but I'll be there every moment.'

'Promise?'

'I have strict orders.' He smiled suddenly and the loft was filled with his brightness. 'Besides, Minstrel, I love you more than any other being in the universe – except one.'

'I know,' she said.

The light faded, and Elmo vanished. Only a tiny glow remained, outlining where he had been. Minstrel heard an echo of her favourite song, as if Elmo were singing from a place she could not see but which was not, after all, so far away. She closed the lid, lifted the chest and went downstairs with it.

Catherine was wrapping some bread and cheese in a small cloth. She put the food and a small leather bottle of water into a drawstring bag, and tied it to Minstrel's belt. Catherine was crying and could not speak. But she held Minstrel close, kissing her cheeks and forehead and hair. Minstrel clung to her mother, terribly aware of Griselda waiting already by the open door.

Minstrel's father made a sling out of soft animal hide and placed the small chest across Minstrel's back. The chest rubbed painfully against Minstrel's shoulders and spine, but Griselda made no offer to help with the burden.

'Goodbye, Minstrel,' said her father, holding out his arms.

Minstrel offered him her cheek to kiss but could not bring herself to embrace him. Then she walked out the open door and into the night. Griselda was close behind her, cold and overpowering. Minstrel heard the door of her home slam. She felt abandoned, unbearably alone, and longed to throw down the chest and race back to her parents' arms. But Griselda's hand was hard on her wrist, the fingers curved like claws, tight and inescapable.

Katerina Mataira

THE WARRIOR MOUNTAINS

ILLUSTRATED BY JOHN BEVAN FORD

Long ago . . . in a magic time
  When mountains walked and talked
There were four warrior mountains
Putauaki, Tauhara, Taranaki, and Tongariro

They were boisterous mountains
Always bickering
Always boasting
And always ready for a fight

Close by . . .
Wrapped in her cloaks of flax and fern
Was the gentle maid mountain
Pihanga

Pihanga was so beautiful
All the warrior mountains loved her

She had grown up with them
Had played with them
And had shared her secrets with all of them

Now . . . each of the warrior mountains
Secretly wished
That Pihanga was his alone

One day . . .
When he thought the other mountains were not looking
Putauaki crept up to Pihanga
And whispered . . .

Pihanga
You are so beautiful
And I love you very much
Will you be my wife?

But Pihanga was not ready to marry
She liked things the way they were
All she said was . . .

Mmm . . . perhaps?

The other mountains were all watching
And they laughed at Putauaki

Why should Pihanga marry you!
They scoffed

Let me try my luck, said Tauhara
And he stepped up to Pihanga

Pihanga . . .
You are so elegant
I love you too
Will you be my wife?

But to him also Pihanga's reply was . . .

Mmm . . . perhaps?

Now . . . it was Taranaki's turn
He stood before Pihanga and said . . .

Look at me Pihanga
I am tall and strong
I will make you a good husband
Marry me

Pihanga looked at Taranaki
Yes . . . he was tall
And strong and very handsome

Nevertheless . . .
She just shrugged her shoulders and said . . .

Mmm . . . perhaps?

Then Tongariro presented himself before Pihanga
And said firmly . . .

Pihanga . . . we all love you
We all want to marry you
You will have to choose

Pihanga protested . . .

I don't want to marry, she said
Can't we stay the way we are?

No! insisted Tongariro
We cannot! You will have to choose!

Yes! echoed the other mountains.
Choose Pihanga choose!

Pihanga was just a little annoyed

Hmph! she said
Very well!

I shall marry whoever is the mightiest of the warrior mountains

I am he! shouted Putauaki
No you're not . . . I am! challenged Tauhara
Move aside friend!
I am the mightiest, said Taranaki
Indeed! scoffed Tongariro
Well . . . there's only one way to find out
We will fight!
We will fight to the last man!
We'll soon see who is the mightiest of the warrior mountains!

And the warrior mountains
Sucked in the hurricane air
Fired their furnace lungs
And hurled into battle

The earth rumbled
The ground quaked
And smoke blackened the sky

Great clouds of ash belched into the sky
Down the mountain sides
Spewed white hot lava
And giant rock missiles
Exploded in the air

The warrior mountains
Locked in battle

The days smothered
The sun choked
The nights flamed with fire

Night followed day
Day followed night
The sun rose
The sun set

But the battle went on

Until . . . weak, worn and weary
Putauaki cried . . .

      Stop! Enough! I give up!

He staggered out from the burning landscape
And limped away to a distant plain
To sleep

The others battled on
Until . . . battered, bruised and blistered
Tauhara cried . . .

      Stop! Enough! I give up!

And he dragged himself away
To bathe his wounds
In a cool stream

Taranaki and Tongariro
Were also badly injured
And growing weak with exhaustion
But they fought on

Night followed day
Day followed night
The sun rose
The sun set
But the battle went on
Until . . . summoning up his failing strength for one last effort
Tongariro picked up a huge boulder and hurled it at Taranaki
Taranaki saw the rock hurtling toward him
He tried to wrench himself out of the way
But too late!
The missile crashed into his side and exploded!
He staggered and almost fell
As a long fracture zipped up his side
A great chunk of rock
broke away from his body
And rolled to his feet
Only then did he cry

Stop! Enough! I am done!

Blind and in great pain
He groped and fumbled about

I can't see! I can't see! he cried

Nearby was a small rock called Rauhoto
He was the friend of Taranaki
And had watched the battle
Now he came forward and said . . .

Come brave Taranaki
Let me help you. Follow me

The faithful Rauhoto
Lead Taranaki away from the battlefield
As they went Taranaki's great weight carved a deep channel
in the earth
And he filled the channel with his own tears

That river is now called . . . Wanganui

Haha! exhulted Tongariro

And a million sparks danced in the night sky

I am the bravest!
I am the strongest!
I am the mightiest
Of all the warrior mountains!

And so . . .
Pihanga became the wife of Tongariro

To this day
They are together
In the land of the Tuwharetoa

The warrior mountains no longer fight or argue
Putauaki and Taranaki stand all alone
A long way from Pihanga
But Tauhara is not too far from her

They had lost Pihanga
But they think of her still

Early every morning
When the mists rise
From the mountains
To join the travelling clouds
Each mountain whispers

Carry my best wishes to Pihanga
And tell her that I love her still

Alistair Te Ariki Campbell

AT A FISHING SETTLEMENT

October, and a rain-blurred face,
And all the anguish of that bitter place.
It was a bare sea-battered town
With its one street leading down
On to a shingly beach. Sea winds
Had long picked the dark hills clean
Of everything but tussock and stones
And pines that dropped small brittle cones
On to a soured soil. And old houses flanking
The street hung poised like driftwood planking
Blown together and could not outlast
The next wind-shuddering blast
From the storm-whitened sea.
It was bitterly cold; I could see
Where muffled against gusty spray
She walked the clinking shingle; a stray
Dog whimpered, and pushed a small
Wet nose into my hand – that is all.
Yet I am haunted by that face,
That dog, and that bare bitter place.

Jenny Hessell

GRANDMA McGARVEY PAINTS THE SHED

ILLUSTRATED BY TREVOR PYE

When Grandma McGarvey
painted the shed,
she didn't use ordinary paint.

Instead . . .   she mixed up a brew in the kitchen sink,
using barbecue sauce and Indian ink.
She threw in a bucket of globulous glue,
and a handful of glitter, all silver and blue.

Then she melted down crayons and mixed them all in
with a dollop of something she found in a tin.
'You have to have just the right colours,' she said,
'before you can paint a shed.'

When Grandma McGarvey painted the shed,
she didn't use regular brushes.

Instead . . . she piled up a stack of assorted things –
straw, some floppy old violin strings,
a feather which Polly had dropped on the floor,
(and some hair that the dog didn't need any more).

Then she tied it all up in a wiggly bunch
with some strands of spaghetti left over from lunch.
'A sensible brush is important,' she said,
'if you're going to paint a shed.'

When Grandma McGarvey painted the shed,
she didn't wear workaday clothes.

Instead . . . she dolled herself up in her Sunday best –
        a polka-dot blouse and a violet vest,
        a hand-me-down skirt which didn't quite fit,
        a pair of old socks which smelled just a bit,
        boots that she'd bought at the army shop
        and a hat with a bunch of bananas on top.
        'Appearances are important,' she said,
        'when you're going to paint a shed.'

When Grandma McGarvey painted the shed,
she didn't make orderly patterns.

Instead . . . she began at the bottom with squiggles of blue
that sparkled like waves under glitter and glue.
She added a wobbly wiggle of white,
and a rainbow that didn't turn out quite right.

Then she covered the corners with dribbly dots,
and noughts and crosses, and splotchetty spots,
(and a strip of silver to cover the streak
where the dog had done something disgraceful that week!).
Then she topped it all off with some musical lines,
and stars, and moons, and zodiac signs,
and a brilliant self-portrait in yellow and green
that she put round the back where it wouldn't be seen.
'It always pays to be modest,' she said,
'when it comes to painting a shed.'

When Grandma McGarvey painted the shed,
she didn't just paint the walls.

Instead . . . she climbed on the roof while clutching the tin
and the lid toppled off with a deafening din,
(and the dog, which was yapping and trying to help,
was hit on the nose and ran off with a yelp).

But the roof was so rusty she started to slide
so she had to stretch out and hold onto the side,
and as she leaned over to grab at the tin
a banana broke loose from her hat and fell in.
'Life is full of surprises,' she said,
'whenever you paint a shed.'

When Grandma McGarvey finished the shed,
she didn't just pack up her things.

Instead . . . she invited the neighbours and half of the street
to a shed-warming party with plenty to eat.
Then Grandma McGarvey explained the designs
and told people's fortunes with zodiac signs.
They played noughts and crosses and join-up-the-dots,
and got sticky fingers from all the wet spots.

And when it grew dark they pulled out some chairs
and lit up the garden with firework flares,
and the adults all gasped and the children all grinned
(while the dog ran in circles and barked at the wind).

And Grandma McGarvey smiled proudly and said,
'Now that's what I call a spectacular shed!'

Janice Marriott

KISSING FISH

PHOTOGRAPH BY JOCELYN CARLIN
LINE DRAWING BY JANINE BROUGHAM

Will things ever get back to normal for Henry?

The evening got off to a bad start. It was John's fault – he'd chosen the restaurant. It was Italian, so I figured I could have my favourite pineapple and ham pizza. Well, can you believe this? In the best Italian restaurant in town they didn't have pineapple and ham pizza on the menu. So Marvin and I had spaghetti. I thought they couldn't mess up spaghetti in a place like this where wine waiters rush around with the bottles wrapped in cleaner nappies than Perky's Bubba wears. Maybe the bottles leak.

I had plenty of time to watch the waiters running around. We had to wait ages for our spaghetti. Ages! At McDonald's the service is much better because you never have to wait. Mum kept saying, 'What's the rush?' but we couldn't tell her about our plans for the night.

Mum was putting on a show of her very worst behaviour. I knew she was fiercely covering up her worry about Gran by being extra loud and lovey-dovey. I've seen it all before. When she was splitting up with Dad she acted in public as though she'd just won Lotto, but back at our place she was angry with me all the time for no reason at all.

John and Marvin must have wondered why she was behaving like a kid. One moment she was laughing like a hyena at every unfunny thing poor Marvin said. Then she was clawing at John's shirt and braying, 'You've still got what it takes!' when he said something about how old he was getting. It wouldn't have been so bad if the food had been decent. I could have turned my chair away, put my plate on my lap and done some serious eating. But the food, when it finally arrived, was disgusting.

The waiter brought these plates of spaghetti with a measly bit of thin red sauce on top, nothing like the thick orange yummy sauce I expected. And before I could stop him, he picked up this shaker thing and shook a stream of yellow stuff that looked like dandruff all over my meal. Then he sauntered away to check whether his wine bottles' nappies needed changing.

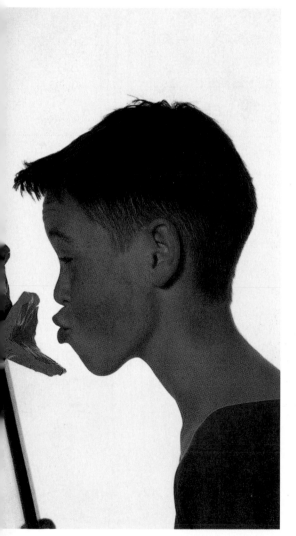

'Looks lovely, dear,' said Mum.

I could smell this dreadful stink, and I looked very carefully at Marvin. It was definitely the smell of vomit. He could have done a quick one into his jersey because he didn't want to disturb us. But no, he was happy enough. John and Mum were yapping away. They weren't vomiting. The smell was deadly.

'Hey, can anyone smell sick?' I asked, looking under the table in case the restaurant cat was chundering on my shoe. Mum said it's probably the parmesan cheese, and poked at my spaghetti dandruff. Couldn't be! This was a posh restaurant. I took a smear of it onto my fork and sniffed. Yuck! The pong! It was monstrous. Why on earth would the waiter sprinkle dried vomit over my dinner? Then I realised, and I was so ashamed. It must be because the waiter hated Mum's loud behaviour. In posh restaurants they wouldn't come over and drag you out the door. Instead they sprinkle vomit on the food of the most responsible-looking person in the group.

The next terrible thing that happened was that Rachel and a guy who could have been a Teen Throb model came into the restaurant. They were laughing and smooching so much they sat down before they realised me and Marvin were at the next table. When Rachel finally looked at us, she gave us a glare that would freeze-dry a nuclear reactor, and they got up and walked out.

It was a pitsville evening. When we left the restaurant

Mum and John said they were full and wasn't it wonderful to eat veal like that? Marvin said he was full because he'd eaten his and mine. The puddings were tinsey-winsey, and Mum wouldn't let me order six of them. I was starving.

Worst of all, they decided we'd walk home instead of taking a taxi. 'It's a full moon,' murmured John. I had to agree with him about the moon. It was ideal weather for the burglary because we wouldn't need torches and I wouldn't bang into anything else and knock all the rest of my teeth out.

When we got inside, Mum and John started dancing. That old-fashioned touching-each-other dancing. I told Marvin they weren't usually like this, but I don't think he heard above the noise. John was playing an Elvis record. Not a CD, not even a cassette, but a black, flat, hole-in-the-middle record. The sort they find in archaeological digs. The song was this funeral hymn thing I think. Very slow and depressed sounding. The guy was moaning, 'Love me tender, love me true.' I couldn't watch.

'Marv. Let's crash.'

'Yeah, man.'

Maurice Gee

Under the Mountain

ILLUSTRATED BY SEVEN
PHOTOGRAPHIC STILL FROM TVNZ ARCHIVES

*Beneath the extinct volcanoes giant creatures
are waking from a spellbound sleep that has lasted
thousands of years.*

They dressed. Soon they had the canoe on the water. Theo
worked it silently along the band of shadow by the shore
line. Rachel sat in the bow holding the camera and torch. No sound
or movement broke the stillness of the lake. Several cars went by
on the road to Milford but they seemed in another world. Rachel felt
the rushes brush her arm. Three houses slipped behind them. She
kept her eyes on the jutting piece of land where the Wilberforces'
lawn met the water. The smell was very strong. She was sure the
Wilberforces were somewhere in the night.

Theo nosed the canoe into the reeds beyond the vacant section. A faint bluish light showed in the Wilberforces' porch.

'That means the door's still open. Quiet.' He heard the creaking sound of something heavy moving on floor boards. A dark shape came down the steps with a smaller one behind.

'It's both of them. Keep as still as you can.'

The Wilberforces moved down the lawn, keeping in the shade of trees. They stopped out of the twins' sight. One, two, three minutes passed. A single cough sounded, a single quack.

'What are they doing?'

'Shsh.'

Suddenly two shapes, one large, one small, rushed from behind the tree towards the lake. They moved with the speed of running dogs – for a moment Rachel thought they were dogs. But the large one was too large. And she saw as they crossed a patch of moonlight that their shape was wrong. They were low to the ground as hedgehogs – lower, as slugs. They slid down the lawn, down the bank, into the water without a splash, and were gone. A small ripple moved into the reeds and rocked the canoe.

She had felt Theo's arm reach round her and grab his camera. 'Too late. Damn.'

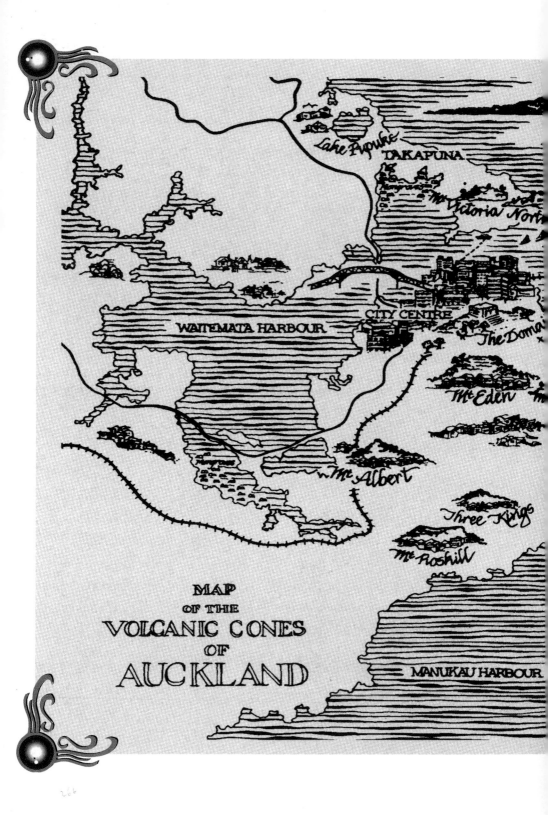

Lake Pupuke

TAKAPUNA

Mt Victoria North

WAITEMATA HARBOUR

CITY CENTRE

The Domain

Mt Eden

Mt Albert

Three Kings

Mt Roskill

MAP
OF THE
VOLCANIC CONES
OF
AUCKLAND

MANUKAU HARBOUR

'What were they?'

'I don't know. But I'm not staying near the water.' He propelled the canoe forward. She clambered along the bow and jumped on the lawn. He followed, splashing in the reeds. Ahead, Rachel ran towards the stone wall at the front of the house.

'Rachel.'

She stopped.

'We've got to look for Mr Jones.'

'He hasn't called again.'

'He might be knocked out. Just a quick look. If he's in there we've got to try and save him.'

She had never been so frightened. But she followed him up the steps into the porch. 'I forgot my paddle.'

'Me too. Give me the torch.' He stood in the doorway and pointed it into the room. A blue light shone out from a small leaded window straight across from him. This was the light they had seen from the lake and from Rachel's bedroom. Round to one side ancient curtains, black and still as water in a well, hung from brass rings on a wooden bar fixed to a lintel. Their heavy dusty tassels drooped on the floor.

Three doors led out. Each was bolted and padlocked. The only other window was boarded over.

That was all – unless . . . Something in the back corner of the room caught his eye. He shone the torch at it. A trapdoor lay open against the wall, with a dark hole leading down.

'If they've got him, he's either down there or behind that curtain.'

'I don't want to go in.'

'We've got to. Come on. The trapdoor first.'

They stepped into the room. At once they were struck by its coldness. Their skin seemed to shrink and the warmth drain out of their bodies before they had gone two steps. Then they felt a stickiness on their feet and lifting them saw their soles were coated with the same grey dust Uncle Clarry had found on his lawn.

'It's all over the floor.'

They crept to the trapdoor. Concrete steps went into the gloom, which seemed to swallow the light of the torch when Theo shone it down.

'I'm going to have a look.'

'No, Theo.'

'He might be down there. You stand at the top and shine the torch in.'

She knew that once he had started on something he would carry it through.

'I'll give you till I count twenty. Then I'm going.' She knelt on the floor and shone the torch into the cellar. Theo went down the steps.

'They're covered with dust. Phew, the stink. Like a dunny . . . Shine into the corners, Rachel.'

In a moment he gave a soft cry. 'There's a tunnel. I think it slopes down. Give me the torch.'

'Theo, they might come.'

'I've got to see in. Hurry up.'

She ran down the steps, her feet puffing up dust, and crossed to where Theo was kneeling in a corner. The mouth of the tunnel was round like a culvert and about a metre across. Rachel shone the torch into it.

'It goes down all right. Just a small slope,' Theo said. 'And it curves out of sight about five metres along.' He reached in and felt the walls. 'It's glass. Some sort of grey glass. I wish we could go down.'

'No, Theo.'

He put his head into the tunnel. 'Mr Jones,' he called softly, 'are you there?' His voice seemed to hiss and whisper and slide down into the dark. 'Mr Jones.'

'He's not there, Theo. Let's go.'

'All right.' He was reluctant. 'We'll have a look behind those curtains.'

Rachel started up the stairs. She shone the torch behind her to light him up. But he turned. He went back to the mouth of the tunnel and crouched, listening.

'There's a noise down there,' he whispered.

'Oh, do come on.'

'It's like a flight of ducks, high up.' Suddenly he felt a puff of cold air from the tunnel. It made his hair whisper about his ears. At the same time he heard a rushing slithering sound.

'Something's coming up. Quick, out.'

She kept the light on the steps until he was up. Then they ran to the door. The rushing sound was closer and the air forced from the tunnel raised dust in the cellar and lifted it like smoke through the trapdoor hole. 'Put the torch on it. I'm going to get a photo.' But Rachel had gone ahead into the porch. She ran back to his side. 'She's there, on the lawn. Mrs Wilberforce.'

A loud sudden quack came from the lake. They peered through the door. Beyond the shape of the woman on the lawn, silver water stretched to the opposite shore. They saw a dark shape on it, close to the foot of the hedge.

'It's the canoe. It must have floated out.'

Suddenly there was a cracking sound, a thrashing on the surface. The canoe vanished.

'It must be Mr Wilberforce. He's pulled it under.'

'Theo, *she's* coming inside.'

'Quick, behind the curtain.'

As they reached it something came with a wet explosion out of the tunnel in the cellar. The twins dived through the curtains and Theo held them with his hands to make them still. He peered through the gap into the room. Rachel stood behind him on tip-toe, stretching her neck to see over his head. Whatever it was that had come into the cellar was mounting the steps. It came up swiftly, with a sucking sound. In the blue light it bent into the room; eased over the top step; undulated towards the door. It was grey, glistening with oil and slime. Its shape was almost exactly slug-like; a little rounder, Theo thought, like a German helmet. It had a white bone beak, a black mouth, perfectly round, that ran like a drain into its body, and two blunt knobs in place of eyes. They glowed with a black radiance. As he watched another followed, then another. They slithered to the door and into the porch.

'What are they?'

'Slugs. Some sort of giant slugs.'

'Oh, Theo, how do we get out?'

'I don't know. One of them's by the steps, I think.'

They turned to face the room behind them. It was empty too. Blue light shone from under a door – the same light that glowed through the window in the other room. It showed a number of flattened piles of dust against the walls.

'Maybe they sleep on those.'

'Let's go. Please.'

'They've nailed boards over the windows.' He spoke calmly, but he was as terrified as her. He felt like curling up in a corner, hiding his head in his arms. But he pushed Rachel's shoulder, moved her towards the door. 'We'll go through there.' They had both forgotten Mr Jones.

They reached the door and listened for a moment. There was no sound on the other side. Theo took the handle. It turned easily. He opened the door with a push.

INDEX OF AUTHORS

ACKNOWLEDGEMENTS

The publisher gratefully acknowledges the following for permission to reproduce copyright stories in this book.

Extract from *Again the Bugles Blow* by Ron Bacon, illustrated by V. J. Livingston, first published by William Collins New Zealand Ltd, 1973, text copyright © Ron Bacon, 1973, illustrations copyright © V. J. Livingston, 1973, reprinted with permission of HarperCollins*Publishers* New Zealand Ltd.

Extract from *Archway Arrow* by Margaret Beames, first published by Scholastic New Zealand Ltd, 1996, text copyright © Margaret Beames, 1996, cover and illustrations copyright © Scholastic New Zealand Ltd, 1996, reprinted with permission of Scholastic New Zealand Ltd.

Extract from *The Bantam and the Soldier* by Jennifer Beck, illustrated by Robyn Belton, first published by Scholastic New Zealand Ltd, 1996, text copyright © Jennifer Beck, 1996, illustrations copyright © Robyn Belton, 1996, reprinted with permission of Scholastic New Zealand Ltd and Ray Richards Literary Agency.

Bidibidi written and illustrated by Gavin Bishop, first published by Oxford University Press Ltd, 1982, copyright © Gavin Bishop, 1982, reprinted with permission of Gavin Bishop.

What Peculiar People! by Dorothy Butler, illustrated by Lyn Kriegler, first published by Reed Publishing New Zealand Ltd, 1994, text copyright © Dorothy Butler, 1994, illustrations copyright © Lyn Kriegler, 1994, reprinted with permission of Reed Publishing New Zealand Ltd and Ray Richards Literary Agency.

Haiku and 'At a Fishing Settlement' by Alistair Te Ariki Campbell from *Pocket Collected Poems*, Hazard Press, 1996, text copyright © Alistair Te Ariki Campbell, reprinted with permission of Alistair Te Ariki Campbell.

Kahukura and the Sea Fairies retold by Pauline Cartwright, illustrated by Te Maari Gardiner, first published by Ashton Scholastic Ltd, 1994, text copyright © Pauline Gardiner, 1994, illustrations copyright © Te Maari Gardiner, 1994, reprinted with permission of Scholastic New Zealand Ltd.

Extract from *Focus and the Death-Ride* by Ken Catran, first published by HarperCollins*Publishers* New Zealand Ltd, 1994, copyright © Ken Catran, 1994, cover copyright © HarperCollins*Publishers*, 1994, reprinted with permission of HarperCollins*Publishers* New Zealand Ltd.

Emily's Wonderful Pie by Jane Cornish, illustrated by Sue Hitchcock-Pratt, first published by Scholastic New Zealand Ltd, 1997, text copyright © Jane Cornish, 1997, illustrations copyright © Sue Hitchcock-Pratt, 1997, reprinted with permission of Scholastic New Zealand Ltd.

Extract from *Bow Down Shadrach*, by Joy Cowley, first published by Hodder & Stoughton, 1991, text copyright © Joy Cowley, 1991, illustrations copyright © Robyn Belton, 1991, cover copyright © Penguin Books New Zealand Ltd, 1991, reprinted from the Puffin Books edition, 1992, with permission of Joy Cowley and Ray Richards Literary Agency.

Tulevai and the Sea by Joy Cowley, illustrated by Manu Smith, first published by Ashton Scholastic Ltd, 1995, text copyright © Joy Cowley, 1995, illustrations copyright © Scholastic New Zealand Ltd, 1995, reprinted with permission of Scholastic New Zealand Ltd and Ray Richards Literary Agency.

Extract from *Shining Rivers* by Ruth Dallas, illustrated by Gareth Floyd, first published simultaneously by Methuen Children's Books Ltd, Great Britain, 1979, and Methuen Publications New Zealand Ltd, 1979, text copyright © Ruth Dallas, 1979, illustrations copyright © Methuen Children's Books Ltd, 1979, reprinted with permission of Ruth Dallas.

The Smallest Turtle written and illustrated by Lynley Dodd, first published by Mallinson Rendel Publishers Ltd, 1982, text and illustrations copyright © Lynley Dodd, 1982, reprinted with permission of Mallinson Rendel Publishers Ltd.

Extract from *Night Race to Kawau* by Tessa Duder, first published by Oxford University Press, 1982, text copyright © Tessa Duder, 1982, cover copyright © Penguin Books New Zealand Ltd, 1982, reprinted from the Puffin Books edition, 1985, with permission of Tessa Duder and Ray Richards Literary Agency.

Extract from *Falter Tom and the Water Boy*, by Maurice Duggan, illustrated by Gwenda Turner, first published by the School Journal; Faber and Faber Ltd, London; Criterion Books Inc., New York; and Paul's Book Arcade, Hamilton, 1958, text copyright © the estate of Maurice Duggan, 1958, 1974, illustrations copyright © Gwenda Turner, 1984, reprinted from the Puffin Books edition, 1984, with permission of Barbara Duggan and Gwenda Turner.

Extract from *Under the Mountain* by Maurice Gee, first published by Oxford University Press, 1979, text copyright © Maurice Gee, 1979, cover copyright © Penguin Books New Zealand Ltd, 1979, reprinted from the Puffin Books edition, 1982, with permission of Maurice Gee and Ray Richards Literary Agency. Photographic still copyright © TVNZ Archives.

Duckat by Gaelyn Gordon, illustrated by Chris Gaskin, first published by Ashton Scholastic Ltd, 1992, text copyright © Gaelyn Gordon, 1992, illustrations copyright © Chris Gaskin, 1992, reprinted with permission of Scholastic New Zealand Ltd and Michael Gifkins and Associates.

The Kuia and the Spider by Patricia Grace, illustrated by Robyn Kahukiwa, first published by Longman Paul Ltd in association with Kidsarus 2 Inc., 1981, text copyright © Patricia Grace, 1981, illustrations copyright © Robyn Kahukiwa, 1981, reprinted with permission of Patricia Grace and Robyn Kahukiwa.

Grandma McGarvey Paints the Shed by Jenny Hessell, illustrated by Trevor Pye, first published by Ashton Scholastic Ltd 1992, four-title series, text copyright © Jenny Hessell, 1992, illustrations copyright © Trevor Pye, 1992, reprinted with permission of Scholastic New Zealand Ltd.

Extract from *The Winning Touch* by David Hill, first published by Scholastic New Zealand Ltd, 1995, text copyright © David Hill, 1995, cover copyright © Scholastic New Zealand Ltd, 1995, reprinted with permission of Scholastic New Zealand Ltd.

'The Tramp' from *Tales of the Mist* by Anthony Holcroft, illustrated by Elspeth Williamson, first published by Methuen Children's Books Ltd, Great Britain, 1987, text copyright © Anthony Holcroft, 1987, illustrations copyright © Elspeth Williamson, 1987, reprinted with permission of Anthony Holcroft and Elspeth Williamson.

Extract from *Denzil's Dilemma* by Sherryl Jordan, first published by Ashton Scholastic Ltd, 1992, text copyright © Sherryl Jordan, 1992, reprinted with permission of Scholastic New Zealand Ltd.

Extract from *Sign of the Lion*, by Sherryl Jordan, first published by Penguin Books New Zealand Ltd, 1995, text copyright © Sherryl Jordan, 1995, cover copyright © Penguin Books, New Zealand Ltd, 1995, reprinted with permission of Sherryl Jordan.

Taniwha written and illustrated by Robyn Kahukiwa, first published by Viking Kestrel and Picture Puffins, 1986, copyright © Robyn Kahukiwa, 1986, reprinted with permission of Robyn Kahukiwa.

'Old Tip and the Hot Water Bottle' from *Uncle Trev's Teeth and other stories*, by Jack Lasenby, first published by Cape Catley Ltd, 1997, text copyright © Jack Lasenby, 1997, cover copyright © Cape Catley Ltd, 1997, reprinted with permission of Cape Catley Ltd.

Extract from *The Runaway Settlers* by Elsie Locke, first published by Jonathon Cape, 1965, text copyright © Elsie Locke, 1965, illustrations copyright © Jonathon Cape, 1965, reprinted from Puffin Books edition, 1971, with permission of Hazard Press Ltd.

The Man Whose Mother was a Pirate by Margaret Mahy, illustrated by Margaret Chamberlain, first published by J. M. Dent & Sons Ltd, London, 1985, text copyright © Margaret Mahy, 1972, 1985, illustrations copyright © Margaret Chamberlain, 1985, reprinted from the Puffin Books edition, 1987, with permission of Orion Books United Kingdom Ltd.

'The Man from the Land of Fandango' from *Nonstop Nonsense* by Margaret Mahy, illustrated by Quentin Blake, first published by J. M. Dent & Sons Ltd, London, 1977, text copyright © Margaret Mahy, 1977, illustrations copyright © Quentin Blake, 1977, reprinted with permission of Orion Books United Kingdom Ltd.

Extract from *Kissing Fish* by Janice Marriott, first published by Penguin Books 1997, text copyright © Janice Marriott, 1977, cover copyright © Penguin Books New Zealand Ltd, 1997, reprinted with permission of Janice Marriott and Michael Gifkins and Associates.

The Warrior Mountains adapted from the Maori legend by Katerina Mataira, illustrated by John Bevan Ford, first published by Te Ataarangi Publications, reprinted with permission of Te Ataarangi Publications.

Extract from *A Dolphin in the Bay* by Diana Noonan, first published by Omnibus Books (part of the Scholastic Australia Group), 1993, text copyright © Diana Noonan, 1993, cover copyright © Omnibus Books, 1993, reprinted with permission of Omnibus Books.

'Autumn Gold' and 'Sands' from *Laura's Poems* by Laura Ranger, first published by Godwit Publishing Ltd, 1995, text copyright © Laura Ranger, 1995, reprinted with permission of Godwit Publishing Ltd. 'Sands' first appeared in American magazine *Stone Soup*.

Extract from *Knitwits* by William Taylor, first published by Ashton Scholastic 1982, text copyright © William Taylor, 1982, cover copyright © Ashton Scholastic, 1982, reprinted with permission of Scholastic New Zealand Ltd.

Over on the Farm written and illustrated by Gwenda Turner, first published by Penguin Books New Zealand Ltd 1993, copyright © Gwenda Turner, 1993, reprinted with permission of Gwenda Turner.

Haiku and 'Bird of Prayer' from *Deep River Talk Collected Poems*, by Hone Tuwhare, first published by Godwit Press Ltd, 1993, text copyright © Hone Tuwhare, 1993, reprinted with permission of Godwit Publishing Ltd.

Grandpa's Slippers by Joy Watson, illustrated by Wendy Hodder, first published by Ashton Scholastic Ltd, 1989, two-title series, text copyright © Joy Watson, 1989, illustrations copyright © Wendy Hodder, 1989, reprinted with permission of Scholastic New Zealand Ltd.

Extract from *Drovers Road* by Joyce West, first published by J. M. Dent & Sons Ltd, London, 1953, text copyright © Joyce West, 1953, reprinted with permission of Orion Books United Kingdom Ltd.

Line drawing on page 139 copyright © Bob Brockie.
Line drawings on pages 105, 106, 170, 183, 262 copyright © Janine Brougham.
Photograph on page 37 copyright © Janine Brougham.
Photograph on page 118 copyright © Pat Brougham.
Photographic still on page 274 copyright © TVNZ archives.

Every effort has been made to locate copyright holders. In the case of any omissions, the publisher will be pleased to make acknowledgements in future editions.